Praise f

SCREENWISE

and Devorah Heitner, PhD

"*Screenwise* is a comprehensive exploration of a timely and important topic, studded with practical tips for parents."

—Wendy Mogel, PhD, clinical psychologist and
author of *The Blessing of a Skinned Knee* and
The Blessing of a B Minus

"For all parents who feel like they can't keep up with today's technology, Devorah Heitner has come to the rescue. *Screenwise* doesn't judge or preach. It is full of empathy and insight, providing gems of guidance based on years of deep research and real talk with real kids. A pleasure to read."

—Lisa Guernsey, author of *Tap, Click, Read* and *Screen Time*;
director, Learning Technologies Project, New America

"Don't let your kids' tech life stress you out. Grab *Screenwise* and get the good news and strategies you need to guide your kids (or let them safely guide you) into a smart and savvy digital life."

—Deborah Gilboa, MD, parenting and
youth development expert at Ask Dr. G

"A must-read for twenty-first century parents! Parenting the digital generation requires complex skills that I frankly didn't have—until now. Empowered by Dr. Heitner's timely book, I feel infinitely more prepared to guide my son and daughter through the advantages and perils of modern-day connectedness. Issues like trust, relationships, security, and balance are handled deftly by an expert who clearly knows the territory and shares her knowledge in a relatable way. Every modern-day parent should read this book. Highly recommended."

—Mary O'Donohue, author of
*When You Say "Thank You," Mean It: And 11
Other Lessons for Instilling Lifelong Values In Your Children*

"Find your way from 'screenworried' to 'screenwise.' It's time to get over your techno-guilt and become a more competent and confident media mentor—an enthusiastic tour guide and mindful role model—for your child in the digital age. In these pages you'll find affirmation, encouragement, a gentle nudge or two about your own media use, and practical strategies to help you become a 'tech positive parent.'"

—Chip Donohue, PhD, director, Technology in
Early Childhood (TEC) Center at Erikson Institute

"Devorah has tackled the challenging, modern issue of raising kids in today's digital world head-on. *Screenwise* gives practical ideas and advice for parents struggling with this issue and really enables them to turn what could be a problem into an opportunity. As an administrator in a highly successful 1-to-1 mobile device school district, I face many of the challenges outlined in this book on an almost daily basis. *Screenwise* will help not only the parents in our district, but also the teachers when it comes to ideas and strategies for truly helping kids thrive in their digital world."

—Carl Hooker, director of Innovation & Digital Learning
at Eanes ISD, founder of iPadpalooza, author of the
Mobile Learning Mindset book series

"This book is full of calming words and constructive suggestions for today's parents who are anxious about their children's immersion in digital media. Grounded in the latest research, it will help parents develop their resourcefulness in navigating what can seem like a worrying new world."

—Sonia Livingstone, author of *The Class:
Living and Learning in the Digital Age*

"*Screenwise* is a practical guide for parents and families trying to navigate childhood in the digital age. Not a 'one-size-fits-all approach,' this book is about gaining confidence and resolve to make the informed, intentional choices that will work best for you and your family. The scenarios and solutions outlined are developmentally on-target for the ages addressed, whether toddlers or teenagers. Heitner possesses a clear and direct voice that will help parents find the path that works for them."

—Jennifer Farrington, president & CEO,
Chicago Children's Museum

"Dr. Heitner offers smart, tech-positive advice for parents on how to be good mentors for children, and on how to best use technology rather than trying to monitor every single online exchange. We appreciate the age appropriate advice on how to balance autonomy and support."

—Tom Vander Ark, author of *Smart Parents:
Parenting for Powerful Learning*

SCREENWISE

SCREENWISE

Helping Kids Thrive
(*and Survive*)
in Their Digital World

Devorah Heitner, PhD

First published by Bibliomotion, Inc.
39 Harvard Street
Brookline, MA 02445
Tel: 617-934-2427
www.bibliomotion.com

Printed in the United States of America

Library of Congress Cataloging-in-Publication Data

Names: Heitner, Devorah, 1975- author.
Title: Screenwise : helping kids thrive (and survive) in their digital world / Devorah Heitner, PhD.
Description: Brookline, MA : Bibliomotion, Inc., [2016] | Includes bibliographical references and index.
Identifiers: LCCN 2016024745| ISBN 9781629561455 (pbk. : alk. paper) | ISBN 9781629561479 (enhanced ebook)
Subjects: LCSH: Internet and children. | Internet—Social aspects. | Internet—Moral and ethical aspects. | Parenting.
Classification: LCC HQ784.I58 H435 2016 | DDC 302.23/1083—dc23
LC record available at https://lccn.loc.gov/2016024745

For Dan and Harold

Contents

x   Contents

Introduction

"I feel overwhelmed by the technology in my sixth grader's life; my daughter is accessing online tools and social media sites I am not familiar with, and I need to provide more guidance in her digital life."

"How do we limit screen time to the suggested one to two hours per day when kids are now using these devices at school for who knows how long? Then they want to come home and unwind for a little, maybe watch TV—but they need to get back on a device to do homework. Limiting screen time doesn't seem manageable or realistic."

"When I was a kid, the broadcasting of programs on TV stopped at a certain time. It forced you to stop watching. I often find myself cruising Facebook, watching dumb videos, etc. Is this what my life has become? What else can we do to reclaim our life and help our kids do the same?"

When I lead digital citizenship workshops for parents, I hear concerns like these in every community. Who are these "digital natives" we are raising? And how is their world different from the one we knew when we were growing up?

There is little consensus about how to parent in the digital age, and it can be hard to talk about these matters without feeling judged. I started Raising Digital Natives as a resource to help parents and educators conquer the confusion they often feel when confronted with the way today's kids process information. The term "digital natives" was introduced by author Marc Prensky in 2001 to describe young people who are growing up surrounded by digital technology. This generation is used to "receiving information really fast. They like to parallel process and multi-task. They prefer their graphics *before* their text rather than the opposite.... They thrive on instant gratification and frequent rewards. They prefer games to 'serious' work."[1]

Some have criticized the essentialist nature of calling people who grew up without these tech tools "digital immigrants" and those who did grow up with them "digital natives." Researchers have pointed out that digital natives can also be digital "naives," who may be clueless about the quality of the information they consume or the ways their own data is being mined.[2]

This book is designed to help parents understand how growing up in the digital age presents some new challenges for kids learning to manage time and navigate relationships and how we, as adults, can offer guidance to tech-savvy kids based on the wisdom of our lived experiences. Thus, when I use the term "digital native," I am referring to the touch-screen generation that has grown up creating and sharing as well as consuming digital content. Today's kids are part of the content-on-demand, everyone-is-a-producer generation. How can we help them become "streetwise" in this new world?

We don't want to mistake digital proficiency for good digital citizenship. Because your kids seem up on new technologies and platforms, you may consider them fluent. This is dangerous thinking.

They may rapidly adapt to apps and online platforms, but they need your mentorship.

The opportunities are amazing for the touch-screen generation. Collaborating, creating, and sharing have never been easier or more rewarding. While the digital divide is still quite real—not all kids (even those in wealthy countries) have Wi-Fi or access to a tablet— parents and educators are grappling with how to help the multitudes of kids who do use digital devices learn to navigate the powerful capabilities that come with smartphones, tablets, interactive games and other applications, and social media.

In countries like the United States, Canada, the U.K., and many others, tablets are saturating the market and even very young kids are using them. According to the latest research from Dubit World- wide, three- and four-year-olds can select their own apps, and many children know how to make videos and take photos by the time they are five. The number of kids who can produce as well as consume content has risen dramatically. This is an important change—it is one thing to operate the clicker and choose your own TV programs or choose your online content, but it is quite another thing to be able to create your own content and share it.

Why is guiding our digital natives through the changing world of technology so important? What's at stake?

• **Relationships.** As interpersonal relationships are conducted more and more in the digital world, is your digital native adept or clueless—or somewhere in between? Skill in conducting relation- ships via digital interaction needs to be layered over a foundation of values—values you can model and teach.

• **Reputation.** With every post, every tweet, and every share, your digital native is creating a persona, even as she is experimenting with her identity. It's a virtual high-wire act, and she's bound to have some missteps. While she can survive her slip-ups, they can be difficult and exhausting to repair.

- **Time management.** The digital world is limitless. Making the right choices about how and where to spend time is harder than ever. Without mentorship and guidance, rabbit-hole distractions could claim large chunks of precious childhood.

The landscape is different now, and the rules are changing rapidly. Our kids need help, even if they think they don't. Even if *you* think they don't. It's up to us as parents (and teachers) to ensure that we are helping our kids develop the skills they need to be "screenwise." If they don't learn these skills, they will struggle in today's—and tomorrow's—world.

Screen wisdom is not operational or functional. It is not about how to keyboard or how to code. Anyone can learn the technical aspects of using apps and devices, with enough practice. True screen wisdom is about relationships. It's about the kinds of connections we can have with one another. It's about trust. And balance.

Nuances matter. These skills are complex. A study conducted by researcher Alexandra Samuel revealed that kids who are mentored by their parents get into less trouble in their digital world.[3] I noted with satisfaction that the digital skills Samuel spells out are in harmony with my own weekly interactions with families. The core skills her study identifies include "compensating for the absence of visual cues in online communications," "understanding the norms and etiquette in different platforms," and "balancing accountability with security."[4] These are complex and critical skills, and many adults are still working on them. Teaching kids how to read between the lines of text, how to respond without becoming overly reactive, how to check in about their interpretations, and how to use context to support their understanding of accountability, privacy, and security in a fast-paced world is a significant endeavor and takes time. The frameworks, devices, and apps are changing all the time and will continue to evolve. But the relationship and time management skills you foster will help your child even as the latest, greatest app fades into memory and something new takes its place.

This book will help you find ways to talk to your children, to be their mentor and support as they navigate the challenges of connected life. And it may help you check in with yourself about your own relationship with technology—and to remember that you are the most important screenwise model for your kids.

CHAPTER 1

Raising Digital Natives

Does it feel like the digital world has invaded your home? Is it the uninvited guest at the dinner table? Do you wish that things could "go back to normal"? Are you overwhelmed by the digital demands in your own life and find it hard to remember a pre-smartphone existence?

Even parents who use technology all day at work—and to manage their personal lives—sometimes worry about the effect it's having on their family life. They long for the days of board games and dollhouses, when things seemed simpler. Even TV, prevalent and ever present in American households, seemed easy to manage by comparison.

First the home computer became an essential—but it was typically located in a central place in the house, so at least we could keep an eye on what our kids were doing. Then laptops added some mobility, so kids (and teens) could use them out of our sight, and it got more difficult to stay on top of things. Now, many kids have smartphones, which means they are carrying the Internet (with all its best and worst uses) with them at all times. Now, many schools are providing students with a tablet or laptop for home and school use, leaving parents to figure out how such ubiquitous technology fits into the bigger picture of parenting and family life. Even parents who grew up with pagers and mobile phones find that social media and new modes of gaming have created novel parenting challenges. Where do we start in preparing to meet these challenges? Let's take a brief look at your home to get an overview.

Family Tech: Curiosity, Empathy, and Creativity

This book is all about making your family the source of tech literacy. That doesn't mean that you have to be a tech whiz, with full command of all devices and apps. It does mean that you will be empowered as a mentor. You will understand the potential of new technologies—and the hazards. You will understand and empathize with the social and emotional experiences of growing up connected. You'll be able to have honest conversations with other parents about these issues, which will help your own family and which other parents will be grateful for. So let's get started.

To live a balanced life in the digital age, we sometimes need to wrest family life out of the greedy clutches of distraction. In my family, I am the most distracted person (and many parents find that is true of them). I am the founder and director of Raising Digital Natives, a resource for parents and schools. Posting to social media, responding to e-mail, writing articles to share on my blog, and the other day-to-day work could easily be a 24–7 job. Whether you are running your own company, like me, or are working in a larger organization, boundaries between home life and work life have never been more challenging to maintain. As parents, we are more accessible to colleagues and clients than our parents were, even when we are with our kids. Our work has access to us anywhere. The urge to check our work e-mail early in the morning or late at night can disrupt work–life balance and family life. And you have to admit, e-mail and Twitter can feel clean and contained, compared with power struggles over snacking and homework, the dishes in the sink, and the other realities of family life.

Of course, connectivity can also benefit family life. For instance, it's easy to stay connected with extended family. But technology separates us as well. How many of us can relate to technology researcher Sherry Turkle's phrase "alone together" as a description of the family's interactions at times?[1]

As families, we need to think about what we are sharing—not just with one another, but about one another, too. For many of us, the family album has migrated to social media, and we rarely even print pictures or share them in any other way. How many picture of our kids should we post? Have we ever asked our kids how they feel about what we share about them? It is time to get curious about this. Some parents are constantly sharing pictures and stories of their kids. We should consider the audience—or really, the multiple audiences, in today's world. We should ask our kids' permission (seriously!). Later in this book, I'll dive into the ways asking our kids for permission can prepare them to use social media wisely themselves.

Today's kids use technology to create media, not just consume it. Looking at what they create and share gives us a helpful window into their culture and world. Our curiosity can guide us to learn more about kids' digital worlds, to understand the pleasures and pitfalls in their day-to-day interactions with one another. Our empathy can guide us to support them as they make mistakes and learn to repair them, and grow resilient about some of the ongoing challenges of connected life. This book will give you some strategies you can use to tap into kids' creativity and your own to cocreate solutions for some of the challenges we face in living digitally connected lives.

Parenting Issues

Let's consider the new landscape of parenting in the age of constant digital connection. Moment to moment, our kids are faced with many more decisions about technology and their digital lives than we faced as we grew up with television, the telephone, and possibly a desktop computer.

When I was typing my college applications on my family's Apple IIe, I was conscious of the fabulousness of word processing (my schoolwork was done on a typewriter), but I didn't have the distractions of the Internet—just the allure of friends and maybe a novel or TV show. Today, our kids have a lot of potential distractions to navigate when they sit down to work. Almost all kids need adult help and guidance to learn to navigate the enticing distractions, get focused, and finish their work.

Your kids' new social world may be a challenge for you as well. Often, it may seem like you can't rely on your own experience as a guide, because (1) your children's world feels foreign to you and (2) it changes so quickly that it's hard to keep up to date.

Whatever our screen-time policies are, we may feel judged by other parents. Because the range of approaches varies so much from family to family, we may even feel judged in both directions: some of our peers believe we are too permissive, while others might think we are too strict or worry too much. The fear of judgment can keep us from talking openly with one another, which deprives us of a crucial resource. One of my biggest goals in writing this book and in leading parent education programs is to encourage parents to speak more honestly about the pleasures and challenges of raising digital natives. This book will help you open up a dialogue with your child, but it can also help open up dialogue with your spouse or other co-parents and caregivers, as well as with other parents in your community. None of us is in this alone: I am raising a digital native, too, and I am right here with you figuring this out.

The more open conversations we can have with other parents in our circles, the better prepared we are to meet the needs of this generation of kids we are raising. This is especially true if our interest in the discussion comes from a place of openness and a genuine intention to help. Simply breaking the ice by saying to another parent, "Sometimes I am overwhelmed by all this technology—where do I start with the rules? How do you guys do it?" could be a great invitation to an honest conversation.

Another fear I hear about frequently is that your children will be outsiders if you as a parent don't keep up. This shows itself in two forms: knowledge of the "next big thing" and tech purchases. If one third-grade classmate has a particular device or app, your child may feel that he "needs" it too. You can probably remember the same urge for the "right" lunchbox or sneakers. The difference is that purchasing a connected device like a smartphone, wearable, or tablet is a much bigger decision: it opens an entire world to your child. You want to make sure he's ready.

If you are in a community where the "latest thing" is a pervasive influence, going against the tide will take intention and resolve. In any such community, there are people who are having modest (even gift-free) birthday parties and showing other signs that they won't be acquiring technology for themselves or their kids to demonstrate visible status. Find those people. Talk openly with your sixth grader about why getting the newest, latest gadget doesn't fit your values.

This is where financial literacy can come in to play—your elementary or middle school children probably have no idea how much certain things cost. If they can relate the price of an item to their allowance, or the hourly wage they earn babysitting, they will find it easier to understand why you aren't running out to purchase something.

Often, a device is within a family's means, but the things the device can do—connect to e-mail, browse the Internet—isn't something the family wants their child to have constant access to. At a certain age, either choice—to buy the device or to put off buying it—can be a *lot* of work. If the majority of your child's peers have a device and use it socially, your child's workarounds may be annoying and time consuming for you (for example, having other kids text *your* phone to make plans with your child). Yet getting him his own device will also be a lot of work, as you can expect to be in regular conversations about its best use. Don't kid yourself: parenting a middle schooler in the digital age takes a lot of effort.

Another fear parents frequently share with me is that their child is growing up too fast. Maybe you don't want your kid on the fast track. Honestly, social media and texting can expose your child to many influences. On the other hand, younger kids (i.e., nine- and ten-year-olds) tend to do "little kid" things on computers and phones. That could be dressing and undressing dolls in the latest fashion, or it could be taking "after" pictures in the toilet when using the bathroom. Maturity is not something we should expect consistently of most nine-year-olds, and when parents and educators are shocked by these behaviors (especially the latter) I ask them to consider offline maturity level too. Kids are kids—a device won't change that.

As you think about moving toward a more intentional approach to mentoring your kids on technology, focus on modeling thoughtful use of it, creating times to be unplugged, and teaching kids ways to repair mistakes. As parents, we get so focused on preventing the bad things we fear will happen when our kids interact with peers via a game, group texts, or social media that we sometimes forget to model how to repair problems. And problems are inevitable. Many digital safety experts say that repairing a digital mistake is like trying to put toothpaste back in the tube—and, as you probably know after surviving the toddler years, it can't "go back in the tube," but the toothpaste does need to be cleaned up!

Kids' Feelings About Parents' Tech Use

Parenting is difficult, for sure. But the new world impacts kids' lives, too. I thought it was worth taking a moment to show you the view from the other side. Here is a set of "Rules for Parents" from fifth graders, who show their feelings about *your* use of technology:

- No talking and driving—I hate it when my mom puts in headphones and doesn't even talk to me on the way home.
- Don't watch TV so loud (and late). It wakes me up.
- I hate when my mom makes me text for her when she is driving.
- No talking on the phone or texting at dinnertime or social time.
- Don't post pictures of me on Facebook without permission.
- Limit phone conversations to thirty minutes ("Sometimes you talk to your sister for two hours!").
- Don't say "Five more minutes" and then stay on the phone (or e-mail) for two hours.

As kids get older, they want less of your time (though they may need you just as much!), but they are more concerned about embarrassment. Seventh-grade girls cringed when their mothers used words like "selfies" or texting slang like "LOL" or "BRB" in conversation.

My workshops and fieldwork with groups of teens and tweens, as well as with younger children, inform my thinking. In this book, I'll show you *their* view as much as I can. They tell me things that they don't always share with their parents or teachers!

What Parents Worry About

I work with parents at schools around the United States and beyond, and parents always let me know that they're worried about "what the kids are doing on there" when they walk into a room and their tween and all her friends are looking at screens. And parents say to me, "I'm concerned that our kids have no social skills. I'm concerned that my kid is addicted to games. I'm concerned that they're double-screening and multitasking to the point that they may not ever be able to really focus on anything. I'm concerned that they're going to take a naughty picture, hear about a naughty picture, or receive a naughty picture and their innocence will be destroyed. I'm concerned that they're going to become cyberbullies, be cyberbullied, or be blackmailed . . . I don't know what they're doing on there but I'm worried about it." Following are some of the things parents are anxious about, given their kids' preoccupation with digital devices.

Are Kids Losing Social Skills?

We've all seen it: kid in a passive posture, device in hand, all attention focused downward. Your child is immersed in a game or some other thing. A full hour (or more) can pass without him moving. He's completely disconnected from the world. Try to pry him away, and you risk a meltdown.

Parents express their worry to me all the time that their kids will become addicted to their devices. They fear that kids will grow up disconnected, alone, and unhealthy. Kids' social skills, they worry, are being shaped by their devices, and not in a good way. This potential is why kids need us more than ever. Their world is a lot more complicated now, and technology is only one factor that is making us aware that kids may need more support learning social skills.

Are Kids Being Supervised Appropriately?

Kids today spend a lot more time closely supervised and a lot less time playing outside until the streetlights go on. Parents are much more involved in actively managing their children's social lives—until, at some point, they can't. When kids start middle school, parents' habit of close involvement can present a huge challenge because kids are now, to a greater degree, left to their own resources to solve conflicts or negotiate other tricky terrain. The transition from parent-managed playdates to social independence ("Here's your phone; have fun texting with all your friends") is a steep hurdle, and one that is loaded with pitfalls for kids between fourth and eighth grade who are navigating this transition along with puberty and all the other changes this age brings. Rather than a slow buildup to navigating their social lives, many kids go from parent-organized playdates to managing their own devices and social lives with no training wheels and little mentorship.

The good news is that there are ways to help kids learn the necessary social skills. The "natural" form of socializing that we grew up with left kids who were shy or had other social challenges to fend for themselves. The idea that all kids need to learn social and relationship skills, which has become a larger part of school curricula, does level the playing field for kids who might struggle in this area, and technology can actually help. But most kids, even very social ones, need some help navigating responsibly the social interactions that a device can bring.

Every family will encounter slightly different challenges navigating this transition, but I believe that parents possess the skills needed to help guide kids and help them get the most out of technology. The devices may facilitate some negative behaviors. Or they may just make those behaviors more visible to adults by creating documentation that would not have existed for previous generations. But we can teach positive behaviors instead, so that kids learn to use their devices in a healthy way. When they do, technology can make a positive impact on their lives—and yours.

Is Peer Drama Increasing?

Many parents observe an amplification of emotions in teens and tweens who are new to social networks. With or without personal devices or social media accounts, "drama" usually begins for kids as they move toward puberty, when they start to make peer comparisons and experience feelings of exclusion. Sometimes, especially when kids are gaming, issues can start earlier, although these may be simple conflicts rather than what the kids call drama. While devices don't cause the emotional turbulence, they can certainly exacerbate it.

There are some ages—and personalities—that are wired for drama. You can probably think of an adult colleague or friend who seeks it out anywhere. Conflict and drama are a part of life—how we handle them is what matters. As a parent, you want to look for signs that your child is thriving and enjoying the drama, or is successfully avoiding or ignoring it. If your child is right in the middle of the spectrum, you have an opportunity to mentor him to be kind and not manipulative. But if the drama is isolating or upsetting your child, you need to be even more proactive in helping him create boundaries.

I'll address social drama in the digital age in greater detail later in this book, but here are some examples of the kind of drama you might see kids create in today's world:

- Taking other kids' phones and sending out mean, stupid, or silly texts from their phones
- Sharing embarrassing or incriminating pictures
- Propagating anonymous rumors
- Trying to start trouble between two friends
- "Innocently" pointing out that someone unfollowed you
- Anonymously asking questions about someone on an anonymous site
- Stirring up conflict via comments on a social media site
- Making oblique references to someone who "shouldn't really be on this group text" on a group text

If such behavior presents itself as a negative, stressful factor in your child's life, you may want to consider helping her plug into another community, scout group, or youth group. Also, it's perfectly okay to unplug! Strategic offline time can be a salve to the chafing of everyday tech-induced issues. While I believe we want to foster positive use of technology, that doesn't mean it needs to be a 24–7 pursuit. Breaks are good. They help us reset—and not just kids!

So ask your child if she has seen other kids being mean in group texts or social media spaces. It happens all the time, so don't be surprised at what your child reports. And most importantly, don't overreact. This book will teach you how to navigate many of these situations and help you determine when to bring in outside help.

Are Kids Failing to Understand Privacy?

A common refrain that I hear from parents is that today's kids "have no sense of privacy!" What this really means is that our kids' concept of privacy is different from ours. Young people today live life more "in the open," sharing information about themselves under a different idea of what is "public." My strong belief is if we choose to be judgmental about this we are missing a huge opportunity to mentor our kids. Instead, we can face reality and help them better manage their privacy.

There is a strong culture of sharing among both young people and many adults now, so we are not likely to eliminate sharing. We want to help our kids figure out appropriate boundaries, of course—there are real dangers to sharing everything all the time. We need to be able to teach our kids how to share in an informed, thoughtful way.

How Kids View Privacy

Kids do recognize that they are in public when they are visiting social channels. I see this all the time in my fieldwork with teens and tweens. Here's how they handle it, though. Kids use code to "create" privacy. They make oblique references that only their clique will understand. That way, they can hang out in public with some privacy—at least their concept of privacy. Yet, they don't want to be invisible—they want peers to be aware of them and their actions. Being forgotten or invisible is of deep concern to them.

I do an exercise with middle schoolers in which they identify different issues on a continuum of how private or public they are, and their responses vary by age and by context. For example, I ask kids about how they would handle family news like their parents' divorce. Most kids in my groups agree that a friend's parents' decision to divorce is not a peer's news to share. They would be mad if a friend shared such news about their family without their consent. However, many did say, "What's the big deal?" Or they said things like, "I'd want to know so I could be supportive to my friend." There is a lot to like about these kids' thoughtful responses.

Safety or Privacy?

My hypothesis based on many conversations with kids is that in the post-9/11 world, kids value safety more than privacy. Students at the high school and middle school level frequently tell me that it would be okay with them if the government were to look at their data because they "have nothing to hide." They also find the reality of retail and brands knowing their preferences to be more convenient than creepy.

We want kids to understand that we trade data for this convenience. Most of the time, we're okay with this. I won't get into whether that's a good or bad thing, but it's important to be aware of it so you can help keep your kids safe. The important thing to understand for now? Kids do want some privacy, but they think of it differently than we do. And sometimes that privacy is from their parents and teachers, and even sometimes from their peers!

Are Kids Creating a Permanent Record?

One of the concerns I hear most frequently from parents is, "Will my kid wreck his career because of some stupid thing he posted in seventh grade?" While it's not likely, the longevity and public nature of the information we share is a concern. We should consider everything we post to be public and permanent. It gives you pause, right?

Schools are varied in their approach to day-to-day concerns about digital privacy, so I would *not* assume your child is learning good practices at school. We need to figure out as a culture how we want to deal with digital indiscretions, but there is no consensus yet. I wish that what you post before you're eighteen, much like a criminal record, could be expunged. At the very least, those posts should be taken less seriously. Chapter 9 addresses how to mentor your child on the realities of her public presence. When kids are little, you are the authors of their digital footprint. Think hard about what you share and post, and once your child is old enough (perhaps between six and eight), begin to request her permission before posting her picture on social media. If a younger child objects to having her picture taken or shared, we should heed her wishes as well.

Are Kids at Higher Risk of Bullying?

Bullying has existed since the playground was invented. Kids will be kids, and sometimes they will cross the line into dangerous behavior. While bullying isn't new, bullies do have novel ways of accessing their targets now that technology has been added to the mix. And we as parents (and teachers) need to understand some of the new ways these behaviors are expressed—and what to do about it.

First of all, just as in the analog world, you need to be able to discern between everyday, run-of-the-mill hurt feelings and more serious behavior (I'll address many of these issues in more detail in chapter 6). How do you know when the danger is elevated? Trust your instincts. Aside from the intensity of the harm, the frequency of the incidents is an indicator that the problem has risen to a level of concern. When your kid is the subject of intense haranguing, threats, or even blackmail, the situation becomes highly emotional. Kids and their parents struggle to resolve these issues.

We need to give kids very clear guidelines for when they should reach out for help. I've encountered numerous stories of kids blackmailing other kids, threatening one another, and worse. We need to be sure our kids can come to us if they feel threatened or are being coerced by others. Let your kids know that if someone tries to harm them, you'll help them. They need to know that your help is unconditional—even if they've broken the rules and are using a social platform you've forbidden, for instance. Their safety is important, and no one is allowed to mess with them! A bully's or abuser's threat, "I'll tell your parents what you've been doing," is less effective if you let your children know that they can always come to you.

Of course, it's up to you as a parent to make rules and set boundaries. There is no uniform set of standards your child's school or local law enforcement will use to handle problems like bullying or harassing behavior among kids. One of the most important things you can do in an ongoing harassment situation is to cut off the harasser's contact with your child. This will keep your child safe, but keep in mind that she might feel like it is a punishment if you are cutting her off from friends.

Realize that your child may not perceive the situation the way you do: "If you tell anyone . . ." is a threat, plain and simple. Explaining this to your child will let him know that he has rights, and that this behavior is aggressive and must be stopped.

Kids are much more likely to be able to deal with the ups and downs of drama and concerns about missing out than with bullying or harassment, but it is important to acknowledge any feelings of ostracism and to take them seriously if it does happen. Some schools are much better at dealing with instances of harassment than others. If the school has supportive policies in place and your child is being treated badly by school peers, you can collaborate with the school to get some help. You might also look for counseling in the community with a social worker or psychologist who has experience with young people experiencing social challenges.

Are Kids Seeing Inappropriate Content?

It goes without saying that the Internet is filled with things you'd prefer your child not see. Violence, sexual content, and other intense, adult-oriented content has no place in a child's world. Our fear that kids will be exposed to upsetting content is realistic, and the issue is bound to come up, even if your child wasn't seeking the inappropriate images he sees.

So, what do you do if your kid sees pornography or other content you wish he hadn't? With very young kids (pre-K to second grade), try not to freak out. Ask your child, "What did you see?" Assure him that you are not mad at him, but you are sorry he saw something "not for kids." Ask, "How are you feeling?" and give him space to talk about it.

This can be a different conversation for different age groups. One parent told me that her six-year-old daughter was shown pornographic content by another six-year-old at a friend's house. This mom told her daughter that she would go to "kiddie jail" if she tried such things, in a panicked attempt to protect her from inappropriate sexual experimentation.

While the mother's panic is understandable, a fear-based response could backfire and actually *increase* the child's interest. As calmly as possible, you should tell your child that she saw something intended for grown-ups and that it is not for kids. Let her know that most grown-ups don't even watch those kinds of videos, and say, "I will help you make sure that you don't see something like that again."

Kids are drawn in by social pressure. The "fear of missing out" (FOMO) is a real thing. This is why you'll want to give them the language to use so they can remove themselves from situations where they might feel pressured to join in. Empower them to walk away, turn the computer or other device off, and say, "That it is not for kids," and "I don't want to see that." It helps to have this discussion *before* a problem arises, if you can.

What If What They Saw Wasn't an Accident?

If your kids are in third to eighth grade or beyond, assume there is a good chance that curiosity led them to find inappropriate content. This can be hard on parents, because we don't want to believe that our children would do such a thing. Remember that it is natural for kids to be curious, and they are learning boundaries. The positive thing is that you've stepped in to help them—at the right time.

It is okay to say, "Adults make content for other adults," and let them know that even many adults feel that such content is not positive, or that it demeans women, or that it depicts a narrow view of sexuality. Pick your own line—you likely have strong feelings about the subject, and it's perfectly reasonable to let that show.

One woman reported that her nine-year-old searched "sexy naked ladies." This is a kid who needs good information, to be told his interest is normal and not aberrant. But this is also a kid who—like all kids—does not need to be doing unsupervised Internet searches.

Deborah Roffman, an expert on sex education, thinks parents should do as much as possible to keep young children away from pornography.[2] Roffman believes that seeing graphic performances that are devoid of context strips sex of its meaning between people. She advises that, if your children do see pornography, you talk to them about how different it is from real sex. She also advises that you talk with your kids about the possibility that they will see "naked people" on the computer, once they are old enough to search, and ask them to come and talk to you if they do.

In *Sexploitation: Helping Kids Develop Healthy Sexuality in a Porn-Driven World,* author Cindy Pierce points out that parents she interviewed claimed their teenage boys don't view pornography, despite research suggesting the average age of initial exposure to pornography is eleven. Pierce says, "Almost all the boys and young men I have interviewed count on their parents' naiveté. Guys share humorous stories about parents bragging to other parents about how much time their sons spend studying in their bedrooms."[3] As kids get older, Pierce shares that it is important to let them know that their sexual desires and fantasies are normal, but that pornography could make it harder for them to enjoy their relationships once they are ready for partner sex.

At one of my talks, a mother told me that her eighth-grade son had become addicted to pornography on his phone. When his parents found out about his viewing, they confronted him and he admitted that he felt unable to stop. In this situation, putting a filter on the phone—and each home device as well—could be helpful in breaking a habit that the boy himself said he wanted to change. Obviously, friends, and possibly even the local library, still have unfiltered devices, but making the constant flow of Internet pornography less convenient might be enough to help some kids in this situation.

No News Is Good News

Whether the material appears on TV, YouTube, or Facebook, there is a lot of content beyond pornography that you wouldn't want your child to see. This has happened to me personally. While I was speaking with a group of parents at a school in New York City, my five-year-old son was staying with his grandfather. He sneaked downstairs while my father was watching the ten o'clock news, and he saw a terrible act of violence that had been filmed by a bystander and replayed on the news, as well as all over the Internet. This video was not something I would have wanted my child (or even an adult) to witness. We talked about how scary it was, and I listened to my son and answered his questions honestly, but in an age-appropriate way. And my husband, my dad, and I all talked about how to be a little more vigilant in the future.

Kids' interests may lead them to unexpected places. For example, a young man I know loves to watch extreme weather videos, but he was unprepared to see graphic video of injured people after a tornado. Because YouTube and other websites can feature graphic violence as well, it is worth asking yourself when your child is ready to operate independently on the Internet. Come up with a plan together for what to do if he sees something scary or upsetting.

Kids Are More at Risk, in General

Lack of understanding leads to fear and suspicion, which is why I'm such a strong believer in giving parents, teachers, and school administrators as much information as possible about kids' digital lives. Information, coupled with a strategy, affords you more power over the difficult issues surrounding life in the digital age. Two issues that many parents ask me about are connecting with geo-tagging and talking to strangers.

Geo-Tagging

Mobile devices have precipitated a huge change in our culture, to say the least. A decade ago, we didn't expect to know where our friends, spouses, and children were at all times. Maybe we could picture our kids at school, walking home, or playing outside, but we didn't know for sure. And when we were eleven, twelve, or thirteen, our parents certainly did not know our whereabouts constantly.

At least, mine didn't...I still remember a police officer asking me if I was Devorah Heitner—I was thirteen and walking with a friend in New York City. My friend and I had gone into the city to celebrate his birthday and were wandering around Greenwich Village like the suburban kids we were, trying on sunglasses and eating dollar slices of pizza. Turns out, his parents were holding a surprise birthday party for him and he was out walking around with me instead! The cops were annoyed but also amused. My friend's parents called the police to find us, but this scenario is unthinkable today—the parents would have just texted their son, in the unlikely event the kid was in an unknown location in the first place!

Not only are we always reachable now, but geo-tagging is a "new" concern as well. With every post, every check-in, and every message about where we are, we are leaving a trail. You may want to know where your kids are, but do you want *everyone* to know where they are? The dangers of that are pretty obvious.

Talking to Strangers

Through social platforms and online games, people whom you don't know may have access to your kids. The Internet makes it easy to be anonymous or, worse, to pose as a child in order to make contact with children. Though this is a real danger, try not to panic just yet. The good news is that, the research shows, most kids don't want to connect with strangers. Most kids, most of the time, want to use technology to connect with people they already know.

But they might not mind playing Minecraft with strangers. They also might enjoy using apps that offer them the chance to speak with people across a wider geographic area, so some apps, games, and sites may potentially be problematic.

The most important thing to remember is that you want to know what your kids are doing with any given app. The app itself may be harmless, but their actions are what's important. With whom are they using the app? What kinds of experiences and interactions are they having?

Clearly, you don't want your young kids on dating apps, hookup apps, and those that are focused on connecting with strangers. Having a policy for young users that any new app needs to be parent-approved seems sensible, but know that kids can hide icons to make it appear that they don't have a particular app. In general, monitoring leads to more monitoring, so talking with them about their app use is often a better way to know what's going on.

The most important insurance against your children having bad experiences is letting them know they can come to you. Even if they have done something they regret, they need to feel that they can talk to you about it. If kids don't feel isolated, they are far less at risk.

When you read stories of kids extorting one another you have to think about how isolated the victims felt. These kids felt that they "had to" do what the aggressor asked, even against their better judgment. We want to help our kids understand that someone who would try to extort you cannot be trusted. The more of yourself you give, the more power you give up, and the more vulnerable you are to continued harassment. This is a critical message to impart, because kids may end up in these situations and have no idea how to get out of them.

Putting Knowledge into Practice

Awareness of digital safety and etiquette is important. Talk with your child and see if she can come up with some reasons why it might not be great to let everyone know where you are at every share. Aside from safety concerns, has she considered the possibility of hurt feelings? Waiting to share certain events and activities is a strategy kids sometimes use to diffuse the sense of exclusion other kids may feel when they are not invited. A simple solution is to turn off geo-tagging/geo-tracking—and for many families, this is a helpful decision.

Invite your children into conversation about how to make the best use of digital devices. What are the issues surrounding technology use? What are the benefits and dangers? How can you make good decisions? What are the family criteria for green-lighting an app or game? What are the criteria for when to be connected and when to unplug and how do they align with your values? We'll get into all this and more throughout the book. While there are a lot of things we don't want our kids to be doing with technology, we will focus in this book on how to live with, and actually *thrive* with, technology day to day. Let's start by taking a peek behind the curtain at your kids' digital lives.

CHAPTER 2

The Kids Are Alright

Kids' knowledge of technology may seem intuitive. After all, they learn it quickly and become fluent in new applications rapidly. But that doesn't mean they see the whole picture. They still must be taught explicitly to use technology for its best purposes—and they are best taught by you.

Here's an example. My five-year-old reorganized my apps into a folder labeled "Grown-Up Apps." The spelling (GROONUPPP) was a dead giveaway that it was his handiwork. Just because he can organize a smartphone interface doesn't mean he is ready to go to the app store and choose high-quality kids' apps for himself, do his own Internet research, or get his *own* smartphone!

Studies show that, for all their fluency, kids still demonstrate a lot of weaknesses when it comes to their tech world. For instance, they don't always know how to evaluate and interpret data.[1] They also have too much trust in the results of a quick Internet search. "Just Google it" may seem like the answer to everything, but as parents, we can help our kids cultivate true digital literacy. We need to help kids understand how to evaluate sources and have a sense of how they should rank a source of information for quality and truthfulness.

Kids learn some digital literacy skills in school, to be sure. Teachers are more tech savvy than they have ever been, but you can't guarantee that digital skills will be a meaningful part of the curriculum. Even in schools where information literacy is emphasized, educators and parents tell me that kids don't always apply those principles in their personal searching and reading. Doing research with your child about a historical or current event, or about a destination where you plan to travel, is a great way to assess his skills in this area.

The good news is that kids want to get this right. They want to create a positive impression and be a good friend in online gaming and social media environments as well as in person. By high school, most of them tell me they want to avoid drama. They are creating content, sharing fan fiction, and using social media in fun and appropriate ways. Let me share some voices of kids to give you a sense of their perspective. And, of course, ask your own kids to fill you in as well. You'll learn a lot!

What Kids Do with Technology

"What are they doing on there?" It's a question parents ask me constantly, expressed as an urgent worry. I've interviewed a lot of kids, and I have answers for you. What they are doing might surprise you. I've taken what I've learned and categorized the activities in four ways:

- They consume (and create) content
- They control their digital world with varying amounts of help/success

- They connect with others—constantly
- They are mean to others—sometimes

Let's look at each of these activities briefly, so you can get a window into your kids' digital world.

They Consume (and Create) Content

While kids may not always be great at evaluating the quality of information they find, they certainly know how to search for it. YouTube is their go-to search engine, and the world-dominating search engine Google (at least at this writing) is also a huge source for kids. Ask your kids to search for something. They'll likely have the answer for you before you finish asking the question! While some kids are consumption junkies, many others create as much as they consume. The tools for creation are so accessible now that most kids are creating. Even five-year-olds can make videos.[2]

While filtering and blocking sites are limited strategies, the YouTube Kids app, which makes it safer and easier for kids to find videos appropriate for them, and tools like Google's SafeSearch or another filter *may* be helpful supplements to your mentorship with preschool and elementary-aged kids. Before you use a filter, ask yourself if your child needs the Internet at all for an activity. A preschooler or elementary schooler can use a tablet for a game or drawing or music application without Internet, and may not need search. If you can't search with your child, does she need to search at all?

Ultimately, you will want to teach your children how to search, so that you can influence rather than control them. They still need your help in figuring out how to find and evaluate information that will be helpful to them. Here are some good starting points to explore:

- Do they know the difference between sites with .com, .org, .edu, and .gov?
- Do they understand issues of copyright and ownership when it comes to online property?
- Do they know how to find images that are available for common use?
- Do they know the difference between what is public and what is private?
- Do they understand the ways websites use pictures and words together to make arguments?

Remember that even digital natives can be clueless about certain aspects of digital life. To get some insight into what kids are up to, I spoke with David Kleeman, senior vice president of global trends for Dubit, a kids' entertainment and research company. Kleeman is also former president of the American Center for Children and Media. He shared Dubit's most recent research, which showed:

- Parents are the primary drivers of kids' media choices until kids reach age four.
- By the time kids are between five and seven, YouTube overtakes parents as the primary influence, though parents remain stronger influences than friends. Voice control gives preliterate kids access to search on YouTube.
- For kids who are ages eight to ten, YouTube is central to searches, and friends are more influential than parents with respect to kids' media choices.
- By ages eleven to fifteen, kids receive more media influence from YouTube than they do from friends. Search engines and the app store are also important resources.

This research can help you home in on where your child and his peers may be getting their media influences, which can help you ask the right questions.

They Control Their Digital World

Young kids are navigating the connected world faster than even their slightly older peers. Their access to the Internet is relatively open, because so many mobile, connected devices are "floating around" even if kids don't (yet) have their own.

It would be convenient if filters and roadblocks stopped kids from accessing inappropriate content, but they don't consistently do this—worse, these tools let parents think, "Okay, I've installed an app: I don't need to mentor my kids." This is why monitoring cannot substitute for mentoring.

They Get Around Roadblocks

It is important to realize that, for some kids, roadblocks are an invitation. The good news is your little hacker may have a bright future if tech employment keeps growing as it has been! Many kids can access anything they want if they have a device issued by their school via computing programs known as 1:1, sometimes written as one-to-one. One mom of a third grader told me that even in the filtered, "locked down" environment of school devices, her son found a back door on Google Chrome and was surfing the Internet in class in his 1:1 school.

Many parents feel that they can supervise what they buy for kids, but that school devices are the purview of school. Kids are savvy about this, and use it to their advantage. "My phone got taken away because I was grounded, but I can do everything I want on my school iPad," one seventh-grade girl told me. The device doesn't matter as much as its connectivity. Once kids have social accounts or other interactive spaces in the cloud, it doesn't matter which device they use to access them.

I don't emphasize kids' ability to get around roadblocks to say it is futile to parent a twenty-first-century kid who will just do whatever he wants; I emphasize it so you can see we have a big job on our hands (I'm a parent, too!), and that putting an app or filter on kids' devices is not enough. We need to equip them with the skills they need to thrive.

Kids Don't Always Love Technology

Kids don't always want the latest gadget or app, nor do they love technology unreservedly. New phone users I've talked with are often stressed by the feeling that they need to be available all the time. Some are critical of technology in schools. While many kids love the easy personalization of learning that can happen in 1:1 environments and the quick collaborations that are possible, others kids are critical. One sixth grader described her frustration with school iPads: "I don't check it all the time—and I hate the updates and constant dings. Our teachers don't know that if you stop us from downloading something, we can get it again if we had it before. It's still in the cloud. Once you download a game, I can go back to the cloud with an arrow. I can get it because I reload it, even if it is blocked."

Another sixth grader at a 1:1 school says, "The teachers think they know what we are doing, but they don't! They are not really teaching anymore—they can submit everything to be graded automatically. School is now just all about them telling us articles to read. We did a lot of PowerPoint last year, and the quiz was just off the notes."

Some kids find distraction to be a huge issue. In the words of Tanya, a seventh-grade girl at a 1:1 school, "Even though they are fun, I sometimes wish we didn't have iPads. I don't remember things, my homework takes longer, it's hard for me to listen and type [at the same time], and sometimes being on a screen just makes me want to get on another screen like my phone."

Not all kids are critical of 1:1 integration. In fact, the kids I've described who are troubled by technology's effects are the exception, but I do think it is important to note that some kids are either ambivalent about the role of educational technology in their lives or are repeating critiques they've heard from their parents. In many schools, I found kids who were very positive about 1:1 computing. A fourth-grade boy in one of my focus groups had been part of a 1:1 pilot in third grade but didn't have a device in fourth grade. He drew a picture of his (now overflowing) backpack and contrasted it with his third-grade backpack, which held just the device and a notebook—his textbooks and worksheets were on the device!

Ultimately, we need to resist the stereotypes that kids love tech for tech's sake. Kids can get frustrated with devices or connected learning when it increases the time a task takes or when it makes them feel they get less personal attention from teachers. They love it when it brings them access to tools they can use to create, learn, share, and connect in new ways.

They Connect with Others—Constantly

Once kids are connected with peers online, those connections can quickly become a constant backdrop. While adults talk about living in the cloud, many kids (and a fair number of connected adults) are living in the crowd. They are on a group text with their whole grade, or they have followers on social media that they know only slightly.

We don't want them to crowdsource their identity from this large and ever-present group of peers.

In this section, we'll hear from them about how they use social media. I'll dive deeper into this issue in chapter 7, which discusses peers and friends.

How Kids Really Use Social Media

Parents often have some grasp of the way adults use social media, but sometimes they don't really get what teens, tweens, and even some younger kids are doing in these spaces. Kids have different reasons for using different social platforms. When asked how kids choose different apps, Mariana, a high school junior I interviewed, summed up some of the uses for various social applications: "Some apps are more for keeping in touch long term. Others are better for day-to-day, like making plans. Some are more about what you are doing right now. Facebook is about keeping in touch with people, having a conversation. Twitter is more like what you are doing at the moment."

Kids text very differently than adults do. Many young texters (and kids newer to texting) are using the feature mainly as a way to stay connected after school via group texts. The initial excitement of group texting is hard for them to resist. While many adults use texting predominantly in a utilitarian way, kids don't have as much pragmatic need. For them, it's more about entertainment, keeping in touch without needing to get together, and being included.

Tobias, a high school junior, told me that his first phone was not a big deal: "I was eleven when I got my first smartphone, an LG smartphone. I thought it was cool that I could have a cell phone. I used it to keep in touch with my friends. For Minecraft, my parents do limit how much I play games, but I can text as much as I want. My sister is a freshman [in high school], and I think she's on her phone way more than me."

Another high schooler, a ninth grader named Daniella, told me, "Social media is where you go after school to review the day's headlines, to see who is doing what, get updates on relationships (i.e., couples getting together or breaking up), or just view day-to-day minutiae. At night, you'll go on Instagram and see what everyone did that day. I follow about 1,200 people and about 1,200 people follow me. We use Twitter for more funny stuff, not really for looking at pictures. I like seeing what other people are doing—sometimes it motivates you to go out. If you see other people out having fun and you are just sitting at home, it makes you feel like going out."

Discussing conflict, Maya, another ninth-grade girl, said, "Most people are nice, but it is good that people are watching out for subtweets—where it isn't always *directly* mean, but it is pointing people toward something that happened, or something that might be not nice about someone. That's mean too, in a way. Some people are pretty harsh, and other people just think, 'Wow, this is interesting drama.' What you put on the Internet is your choice, though."

Fear of missing out—FOMO in shorthand—is a common by-product of kids' social media habits. When I asked about this phenomenon, Natalia, also in ninth grade, said, "Usually I don't feel left out. But some people do too many stories about themselves and pictures with a million people. It is better that you don't look at them more than once. Sometimes seeing that other people are out doing fun things motivates me to go out, but if you feel bad already it can be a little depressing."

Digital Images As Social Currency

Our kids are living in a world where they're constantly photographed by one another and even by themselves (in photos popularly known as "selfies"). It can be hard to understand the way kids—and even many adults—think about their public personas. Our children will never think about privacy the way we do. When kids take pictures of other kids and post them without permission, or when they tag a photo on Facebook without the subject's consent, we may view it as an invasion of another person's privacy. We can cultivate a culture of permission by asking for and obtaining consent, but we probably can't expect to cultivate a reticence to share.

Our kids live in a photo-taking culture. Try not to pass judgment, no matter how you feel about it. In a recent documentary, *#Being13* [per http://edition.cnn.com/specials/us/being13], the subjects talked about taking lots of selfies. Mocking kids for taking selfies or pathologizing the practice misses the point. Kids take selfies to remember moments—the photos act as a visual shorthand.[3] Selfies and other pictures are a reality of their world, and it's not going to help you to fight it.

Young people can communicate much more with a photograph than we might imagine. In *The App Generation,* professors Howard Gardner and Katie Davis report that kids are becoming more literate with images than they are with text.[4] Their interpretations of the photographs their friends post are all about context—shared experiences, places with meaning, styles that signify identity. Kids are very aware that there is a wide audience for a photo shared on social media, and their intended meaning may be intended for a small slice of that audience.

They Are Mean to Others—Sometimes

Kids can be mean to one another (that hasn't changed since we were kids)—and I'm sure you see evidence of unkindness all the time. Any space where kids can hang out online, just as with in-person spaces, you'll find kids being mean.

Groups of third and fourth graders have outlined to me that kids can be mean when playing games. Older kids talk about exclusion and people not wanting to play with them at all. Social media interactions can be spaces for subtle meanness (even non-commenting can feel hurtful) or direct cruelty ("You look terrible in that outfit"). Sometimes you'll find mean behavior in spaces you wouldn't expect. For instance, kids can be mean while working on collaborative projects on platform like Google Docs. Jon Stoper, head of IT at an K–8 school, says he sees kids interacting negatively on Google Docs, Edmodo, and other school-related spaces where kids can hang out. Micro-battles can erupt, or kids will try to one-up others. They may call out an idea as "stupid," sometimes intentionally and sometimes without thinking. Does this mean we should ban digital collaboration? Of course not! But when we see this kind of behavior, we need to give kids do-overs, and if kids hurt their peer's feelings, we need to focus on helping them repair.

What Kids Think They Know

You can see the confidence kids have with their devices; they navigate new apps and new devices with ease, as if they've been using that technology for years. It can be intimidating for those of us who grew up when technology came packaged with users' manuals. We may feel like we can learn a new piece of software, but it seems to take us longer than it takes our kids to do the same task.

Just because they are good at using devices doesn't mean that they know everything, however. When it comes to the technology itself, kids may know a lot. For example, they know that it is very easy to lie about your age online. And that it is easy to create multiple accounts. They also understand that the actions of a small number of kids in their grade are followed by everyone and that others are followed by no one. They know you can play games with strangers, and that you can share games with others. They realize that, even if they don't have a certain game, if they have the right system, a friend can share the game.

Sharing games, getting around roadblocks, lying about your age to gain access to age-thirteen-and-up applications, using your parents' password to download apps, and other tech-related workarounds are much easier than getting a fake ID in high school or college. These "transactions" don't happen in person, and it's much easier to create a facade in the digital world. At an early age, kids get good at manipulating technology to serve their purposes. But there are a bunch of things they *think* they know, but don't. Here are a few examples, by no means meant to be comprehensive.

They think they know how to deal with peer conflict. In my workshops, fifth and sixth graders tell me that if they inadvertently (or even intentionally) spoil a confidence by sharing a friend's news inappropriately, the best way to get out of it is to "spread some lies" so no one will know what is true and what is not. They also "trade" infractions. If one kid betrayed a friend's confidence, he might "let the friend share" one of his secrets. In fact, neither of these is a great problem-solving strategy. You and your child could brainstorm possible solutions. When I ask ninth graders how to handle conflicts with friends and classmates, their answers are much better! So as they mature, kids *do* get better at solving social challenges. As parents, we should support this growth.

They think they know how to manage group dynamics. Lilah texts Monica to say, "What do you think about Sarah?" Monica says, "She's OK, but a little boring." Sarah and Lilah turn out to *both* be looking at Lilah's phone. Monica feels horrible, of course. What started as innocent chatter ends in hurt feelings, and possibly a damaged friendship. There are so many variations on this story, where the audience is not who kids think it is. Kids are still learning how to communicate effectively, and group texting presents some difficult challenges because they must talk to more than one "audience" at the same time.

They think they know privacy settings, but they don't always do such a great job setting them. Depending on their age and maturity level, many kids think that what they post is private. They don't recognize that isn't necessarily true. In my workshops, I've used Geofeedia to pull up images kids had posted that day when they were at school. They were horrified—they had been busily uploading images to various social applications with geo-tagging turned on! The posts were, for all intents and purposes, public. Anyone searching for posts from the school's location could see the geo-tagged posts. If that sounds creepy to you (or your child), then apps like Geofeedia are a great conversation starter.

They think they know how technology works, but may be oblivious to the data trail they leave. School leaders have told me that within the Google Apps for Education suite, kids collaborate using Google Docs and video chat with one another via Google Hangouts. Part of the collaboration is leaving comments for other kids, and many students make the mistake of thinking that these comments are untraceable. Jon Stoper, the educator I mentioned earlier, says that kids are often surprised when he confronts them with evidence that they were using a classroom app as a vehicle for saying unkind things to a classmate.

They think they know how to use apps properly. Even the kids who understand that images in apps like Snapchat (and other "disappearing" apps) can be saved may forget that fact. When kids are in the moment, they sometimes behave as if they don't remember the capabilities of the app—or the workaround that allows a person to save an image or post. They simply may not think of all the reasons someone might save a chat. For example, if they posted something they thought was funny but another kid got his feelings hurt, the child who is offended might save the image to show an authority figure.

They think they know how to avoid plagiarism and cite sources properly. Everything is free on the Internet, right? Wrong! This generation has grown up with unfettered access to information. Today, you can look up anything on any topic. It's all out there, and much of it is absolutely free. This free flow of information has undoubtedly had an effect on the way kids think about intellectual property. It takes a lot of effort to explain to them that, even though an image or a piece of text may be available for free, they can't simply scrape the text or image and use it without permission—or worse, claim credit for someone else's work!

They Have Savvy, but You Have Wisdom

Parents are stressed about the role of connected devices, games, and apps in their kids' lives because they know that the rules have changed, and they feel like outsiders or that they are not "with it." It is natural to feel like you can't keep up with all the latest trends. Perhaps you bought your daughter a music and gaming device, only to learn she can also text her friends on it—and maybe you made this purchase before you were prepared for your third grader to be texting. Or perhaps your son asks you about an app and it sounds harmless, so you greenlight a download—but it turns out that it is filled with in-app purchase "opportunities" that are costing you extra money. Many parents admit to me that they don't know how to get rid of an application once they have downloaded it, even if it turns out to be a bad idea.

While you don't have control over everything your child does, you can be proactive—and intentional. You can set kids up for success both by mentoring your child about responding to different situations and by organizing devices and unplugged areas in your home to encourage family members to engage with media thoughtfully.

Parents are often in denial about their own wisdom. Our kids may act like they know everything—and they can be very dismissive about our knowledge of the world. But even if kids don't see it until they have their own children (*that'll* teach them!), we know a lot.

We know how it feels to be left out. We know how it feels to have a friend leave us behind and join a new group of friends, or to make that transition ourselves. We know what it's like to have a fervent secret crush, or to have a hobby we don't want to be judged for. We know how it feels to have something we said taken out of context. Most of these experiences will happen to our children as well, and some of these situations may be exacerbated by digital connectivity, group texts, and social media.

Your child may feel left out after seeing a friend's photo posted or hearing about a group text he wasn't included on, but the fact that you didn't have these exact experiences when you were his age doesn't mean you have nothing to offer. Because you are in possession of a rich history of lived social experiences, you can offer the help that technology can't. We need to get really curious about kids' day-to-day experiences. We need to ask them what they're thinking, and we need to cocreate solutions with them that take advantage of their creativity and our wisdom.

The most important thing you can do is to trust yourself and realize that your knowledge about your kids and what they need trumps other people's opinions on the matter. Whatever you do, don't just throw up your hands and give up. Social media platforms were not designed around your needs as a parent. They are designed to connect (and to learn our preferences and tastes)—but they don't adapt thoughtfully to different ages and stages of life! As the most important adult in your child's life, it is up to you as a parent to shape his relationship with technology and curate the media he interacts with as much as you can, while equipping him with tools to make good decisions when he is out in the world—or connected to the world from his own device.

As you read, you'll find suggestions for ways to talk directly with your kids about their online presence and experiences. But first, let's assess what you know about their digital world.

CHAPTER 3

Assessing Your Own Digital Literacy

Now that we've looked at kids' digital worlds, what about our own? You may be comfortable at work with spreadsheets or at home with online banking, travel planning, or blogging, tweeting, and Facebooking. Or you may have a more modest tech presence and predominantly use e-mail. Your child uses (or wants to use) social media in a way that is very different from the ways you engage online. Even if you are using tech extensively, you probably approach it differently than your child does.

For many kids, a personal device feels like an extension of their bodies. Parents often express to me that they have a hard time keeping up with the ever-changing landscape of online games and social media, and don't understand the ways their kids engage with these things. What's worse, parents often feel as if they don't know enough to ask the right questions so they can get started. After all, how do you know what you don't know?

As with learning anything new, digital fluency starts with baby steps. New information can feel overwhelming, and sometimes I need to sit with these feelings before I can get curious. If you know that this is your pattern as well, embrace the overload. Steer right into it. Then, when you have a moment, start looking for information that you can approach in manageable chunks. You owe it to your family not to give up at the first hurdle!

Parents' New Role As Media Mentors

Ultimately, *Screenwise* is about mentorship. I strongly believe that this is the best way to prepare your kids for their online—and offline—future. Helping them make good decisions is a better and more effective strategy than trying to protect them from everything that is out there. But being an effective mentor in the digital age means that you need to engage with kids' technology. You need to play what your kids play and lead them into screen engagements that emphasize creativity over consumption. You'll be ready to defeat your whole office in Clash of Clans or Agar.io! Or you may find that video games are hard, and you'll gain a new appreciation for your child's talent.

Diving into your children's pursuits will illustrate that not all screen time is equal. Finding your own mentors will be crucial. Is there a parent in your circle who is an avid gamer and might be able to help you understand the different modes of Minecraft? Do you have a friend or colleague who is an early adopter of new social apps and can tell you about the app your thirteen-year-old is asking for? A mentoring approach, together with an open, curious attitude, will go a long way toward cultivating a positive family life in the digital age. Finding your own mentors in response to specific needs is a great way to go. If your kid is not all about games, you don't need to learn about them right now.

How Do You Feel About Technology?

Let's start with you. What's your approach to technology? Your personal beliefs about media, mass culture, and technology can influence your assumptions about what constitutes quality. As the authors of *Tap, Click, Read*—a study of how early literacy is being shaped in the digital age—have pointed out, the app store is a Wild West, where almost anything may be classified as "educational," including apps that do kids' homework for them or are otherwise contrary to what most educators and parents would want for kids.[1]

So it isn't surprising that parents are often confused when they try to decide what kinds of technology play a positive role in their kids' lives. Not only is keeping up with all the new apps and games difficult, but everyone from grandparents to teachers to other parents may offer a different, and sometimes unsolicited, perspective. These mixed messages are often laden with guilt.

Some promising new research supports mentorship over limiting (or ignoring) what our kids do and hoping for the best. Technology researcher Alexandra Samuel found in a recent survey of seven hundred American families (from a data set of ten thousand) that families employed three main approaches to technology:[2]

1. "Limiters" predominantly use a restrictive approach to screen time without meaningful interaction about the nature and quality of kids' tech engagements. Their approach is "less is more," and Samuel found that, especially among parents of preschool kids, this approach is common.

2. "Mentors" engage with their kids about technology. These engagement activities include "play a video game with my child,"

"talk with my child about how to use technology, the Internet, or a specific website responsibly," and "show my child a book, article, video game, or program to help them learn about technology."

3. The third group of parents are "enablers," taking a more laissez-faire approach. They do not limit, nor mentor—and the kids are left to their own devices.

Samuel's interpretation of her research suggests that while limiting screen time may have some benefits, this technique on its own does not prepare kids for the amount of tech-mediated interaction in our real lives. "Shielding kids from the Internet may work for a time, but once they do get online, limiters' kids often lack the skills and habits that make for consistent, safe, and successful online interactions," Samuels says. Her study found that the children of enablers, with their unfettered access to devices, apps, and games and low parental engagement with these powerful devices, also struggled and sometimes ran into trouble. The best outcomes were from families in which parents actively mentored their children on how to interact in digital spaces, giving their children more realistic and useful preparation for the real world.

Hell Is Other Parents

As you assess your child's environment and her experiences interacting via devices day to day, you'll find that the choices made by the parents of your child's peers inevitably come into play. One mother, Rachel, described the way other parents' choices and the school's policies left her feeling as though she had little control over her child's media use: "My daughter was in fifth grade last year. And, much to my surprise, there was a lot of cell phone use, and kids were starting with social media and texting, and the parents were navigating and not really knowing what to do or how to handle it, and some kids were into it, some kids weren't into it, some kids had phones, some kids didn't have phones, some kids were using it on their iPad—or, iTouches. And then the school started talking about 1:1 initiatives in the school, and that every kid was going to get an iPad. So, as a parent...you have no control."

Another parent expressed his frustrations this way: "I have concerns about how other parents' rules for their children differ from ours. I am concerned about lax parents who don't supervise content when my child is at another home."

Even if you feel like you are relatively in control of your own domain, social pressures complicate everything. Did your child's friends all get Xboxes for Christmas last year? Does it seem like her classmates all got smartphones in fourth grade? Do your kid's peers all seem to have access to the Internet on a desktop in the basement with no parental input? This is tricky territory, to be sure. Maybe you've decided that your twelve-year-old can handle social media and allowed her to sign onto a service and fudge her age—and other families are looking at you as a bad influence!

In my work with families, I see how hard it is for parents to talk with other parents about their experiences. Instead, there is a lot of internal judgment and negativity, with little consensus. If we all strive for open communication about parenting and technology, and take a community-oriented approach when we are concerned about children's behavior, we'll all benefit.

If your older child is claiming to be the last among her peers not to have a cell phone or another device, you can strategize with her about other ways to maintain contact with her friends. You can make the acceptable timetable for getting a phone clear to her, and let her know any conditions you have. For instance, maybe you will want her to achieve a certain a trust milestone before you grant permission for the purchase. Maybe she will contribute financially to the monthly plan, or adhere to certain rules about the phone's use?

In any case, feel confident about your decisions as a parent, and don't let them be driven by others. They are your choices, based on your values, so don't let others take these important decisions out of your hands.

Dealing with the decisions of other parents can be difficult. We can seek to find out why they feel the way they do or to understand their criteria for decisions regarding digital matters. We can search out a more compatible social circle, but at a certain point, our kids choose their friends and we don't have much control over that. It is inevitable that your kids will come into contact with new parents and new rules, and possibly acquisitions that influence you and your family.

Sometimes parents write to me with concerns about other families. Here's a note I got recently:

Friends of ours allow their grade-school child unlimited access to computer games, which the child likes to play. They claim that the child gets aggressive when the privilege to use a computer is taken away. We noticed the iPhone substitutes for the computer while in a social setting. We feel the child is addicted to the device and that the whole family may need professional help to resolve the problem. Can we be correct in our observation? Can computer addiction become an issue at an early age? What can be done for families like this, and whom would they need to approach for help?

We can't control others, so how do we deal with such situations as they relate to our own children? What do we do when we feel there is something truly unhealthy going on? When our kids are very young, we can hang on to some control. If we know that our younger kids may be exposed to experiences we don't like on a playdate, we can tell the supervising parents, "I get freaked out by shooter games, and we'd rather that our kids not play those particular games," or "My kid gets nightmares if she sees a scary movie, so we keep her away from those." We can also teach our kids to say, "I am not allowed to do that at my house, so I can't do it here," but some kids will have a hard time asserting that boundary.

Teen learning expert Ana Homayoun finds that sleepovers are often the place where the worst group decisions are made.[3] Thus, even parents who are otherwise fairly liberal with technology might decide that unplugging everyone at a sleepover (by storing devices elsewhere, perhaps) is a good idea.

With younger kids who don't circulate in the community on their own, you may wish to take control of the location of playdates or other social events. If a problem has occurred at your child's friend's house, and the parents aren't showing concern or forming a plan, you may not be able to convince the parents to change their behavior. The simplest solution is to entertain the kids at your house instead, so that your child is not in an environment you don't approve of.

You may not wish to put your child in a position where he must say no to what is offered, whether that is a single-shooter game or unfettered Internet access and lots of time to search inappropriate content. Peer pressure is still peer pressure, just as you remember it from your own childhood. Some kids are good at self-advocating and some are not. Depending on your child's age and personality, staying within the boundaries you've set may not be a realistic expectation to place on him. This is where you can step in and use your skill and wisdom to help. You could arrange playdates with this friend at the park or at your house if you feel like the child's house is trouble waiting to happen.

Older children who are traveling independently to friends' houses need to be equipped with good judgment and the street-wise/screenwise sense to stop if something doesn't seem like a good idea.

Do You Feel Behind the Curve?

Many parents I work with feel behind the curve when it comes to technology. Let's face it, kids almost always know about the latest trends in technology and social media before their parents do. That's okay.

The big thing to remember is that adults have more social wisdom than their children, even though children are digitally savvy. This wisdom is immensely valuable and should not be underestimated. Why does your child want to text? What is behind her impulse to use a social app? Are there other ways to have some of that connection? What about starting an account together? One creative mom started an Instagram account for the family dog with her eleven-and-a-half-year-old daughter. They only posted together, and mostly followed family members. This gave them both a chance to learn the app, so after a year and a half, when the daughter turned thirteen and was old enough for her own account, the mom knew the app well and had seen her daughter's decision-making process about what to post. This is a great way to use digital "training wheels"—support to help beginners feel confident and avoid accidents as they learn new skills.

You Can Learn from Your Kids

Whether we like it or not, our kids are digital natives. We can't do anything about that, so let's deal with it instead, openly and honestly. You can establish a family culture around technology, and once you start to learn about your children's digital world, you won't feel so estranged from their tech-involved lives.

Take an interest in what your kids do in their digital lives. Learn together with your kids. Play Minecraft with them or share photos on Instagram with them. Show them what you are doing online and ask them for advice about your Facebook posts or LinkedIn profile. Your goal is not to become an expert in technology but to get a window into how your kids think about, and interact with, technology.

The Greenlighting Process for Apps

You don't have to know everything. If your kids ask for an app, these steps can help you evaluate whether it's something you want to allow.

1. **Start by wading in.** Invite your child to tell you everything she knows about the app and to explain why she wants to install it (besides "all my friends have it"). What is the attraction for her? How will she use it? Is it a social app? A game? How much personal information is shared? How do people act in that space? How does it make people feel? As a prerequisite to downloading or purchasing an app, you and she will sit down and interact with it—together.

   Consult a local "expert" for advice. This can be anyone—an older kid, the babysitter, your college-age niece. Find a reliable young person a few years older than your own kid to give you the lowdown.

Also check my website (raisingdigitalnatives.com), CommonSense Media.org., and other online resources.

2. **Go deeper.** Invite your child to explore the app with you so that you can fully understand the terrain your child wants to enter. You can also do some independent exploring without your child. **For games:** Check out the game without buying it. Play a trial, go to YouTube and watch some gameplay videos with your kid, and read user reviews on Amazon. **For social apps:** Check out the YouTube channel for Musical.ly or use the desktop version of Instagram or Snapchat to research these apps. Try searching for monkeys, kittens, Justin Bieber, or try something naughtier—what might your twelve-year-old search for? Know what's out there, but don't assume that just because the major social media apps have porn on them somewhere, your child knows this when he asks for an account. More likely, he wants an account so he can hang out with friends in this new social space.

3. **Engage.** If you are thinking about giving the thumbs-up after doing your research, here are some questions to discuss with your child:

- Ask your child to show you an account or feed on the desired app that he thinks is inappropriate and one he thinks is smart and cool.
- Work with your child to generate a list of dos and don'ts for the new app.
- For a social app, what are the criteria for connecting with someone?
- What is the potential for drama? Can she give an example of how to avoid drama?

- How much time will she be allowed to spend using the app, and under what conditions?
- What privacy settings will he use?
- Is sharing her password with you a condition of use? Must she be "friends" with you, or allow you to "follow" her?
- How will he decide what he will and will not share?
- Does she know how to avoid "geo-tagging" herself, leaving a trail of data?

Wading in, going deeper, and then having an honest discussion with your child is a great way to keep up with the apps she's using and make sure that what she downloads is safe and fun. If the app seems to be dialing up the stress, taking away from other pursuits (sleep, homework, family time), or having other negative effects, then it is time to rethink it.

There are a bunch of ways you can stay informed without getting a master's degree in social media. Have everyone in the family demonstrate his or her favorite apps—maybe make a family "show and tell" event. Spend some time with your kid at the app store evaluating apps. Search for a tech "life hack" that will save you time and energy. If an app or game is frustrating and tends to put your kids in an angry mood, you can jointly cultivate a solution (possibly avoiding that game or even jettisoning it). Or, they could plan to use it only when there is a buffer zone to let off some steam afterward. This is a great opportunity for you to talk through digital issues with your kids, while you're having fun as a family!

Have them help you set up a Twitter account and seek out and follow other people in your field. Many educators are calling this way of learning from colleagues on Twitter a "personal learning network." How can you model the idea of a personal learning network for your children? Explore for yourself to see if any particular platform supports your interests. If your kids are on Twitter or another social app, you can help them follow people whose posts support their interests.

Another way you can cultivate digital awareness is to do an Internet search using your name as keywords. Do this when you're not logged in so that you can see what others see. Alternatively, you can set up an Internet alert (try Google Alerts, for instance: google .com/alerts) for your own name, and the engine will let you know you whenever you are mentioned online. It's not a bad thing to know what information is available about you. You might be surprised. From court proceedings to the price of your home, many details of your life are probably on the Internet.

Doing this exercise with your kids can illustrate for them the issues around leaving a "digital footprint," which I'll cover in greater detail in chapter 9. Lecturing them about technology won't work. Exploring the digital world together will help show them potential pitfalls—and, even more importantly, will create a two-way discussion. Your kids will feel like they are in it *with* you—that you are on their side.

So don't be nervous. You don't have to go all in with regard to technology. You just have to learn enough to understand your children's world and engage with them about it.

Get Curious: Ask for Yourself

As you start to learn more about your kids' world, get as specific as you can. For instance, see if your child can articulate to you what spaces, sites, and apps are useful for different modes and categories of communication or socializing. Ask:

- Why is texting a great way to make plans?
- What areas are the biggest time suck?
- What parts of texting seem to generate conflict?
- If you wanted to keep something more private, where would you share it?

Probe the obvious. Don't play dumb; just tell them you are doing some research.

Don't Panic

Whatever your kids are doing online or with their apps, it's likely not as bad as you fear. What about the problems you hear about from friends or in the news? We all hear horror stories about how the Internet, social media, and smartphones are ruining our children. The good news is that kids are more in control than you may think. Yes, they need your help and guidance, but they generally have a sense of right and wrong.

Let's look at the concept of friendship as an example. I talked with a group of third graders, who suggested that a good friend has to: (1) be kind; (2) make you feel good when you spend time with him or her; (3) be trustworthy; and (4) be fun to play with. When I asked them what makes a friend good to play video games with, they had similar responses.

Kids know what kind of people they want to be. When I asked what makes someone *not* good to play video games with, they talked about someone who cheats, breaks your creations, and can't lose gracefully.

These observations suggest that kids know what they are looking for and that their face-to-face friendships inform their standards and expectations for digital interactions. They also know a surprising amount about safety. For example, when a stranger asks to play video games with them—which is possible on many connected servers, networks, and platforms—they knew not to say, "I am not allowed to play with strangers," because that is a dead giveaway that you are a child! On the other hand, some kids will be better at maintaining good boundaries than others. These are all opportunities for mentorship.

Safe Gaming

If your child is playing video games with people he doesn't know, it is important to go over the rules you expect him to abide by and to recognize that gaming involves an interactive community space. Whether it is an online game such as Minecraft, a console game system like PlayStation or Xbox, or another gaming platform, users can chat and connect. Your child should not reveal his real name or age. People can chat privately with each other in many gaming systems. On some systems, you can select who a player "hears" by choosing options such as "everyone," "friends," or "no one."

Any specific information I can offer on different gaming systems will likely change by the time this book is in your hands. I strongly recommend that you: (1) talk to other parents who have the system your child is using or whose children have played these games to get a sense of what to watch out for (2) search for up-to-date videos and how-to articles on safety with the particular system or game and (3) play with your child, or at least spend time in the room with him when he is playing—with the game audible so you can get a sense of who he is interacting with. Give your child some examples of situations where he should come to you immediately (i.e., someone asking personal questions, wanting to meet in person, or using threatening language).

Overall, observe your child's experience. Is she invigorated by gaming or stressed by it? Does it seem to be supporting her interests and friendships or getting in her way? If something isn't working for your child or your family as a whole, work out solutions with your kids.

Criteria for Making Decisions

Do you feel as if you are making digital-related decisions in a vacuum? Don't be afraid to talk with other parents—start with people you know well. But I encourage you to also talk with parents you don't know quite as well. Ask them their thoughts—it can be helpful to get a perspective that hasn't been formed in the echo chamber of your own social circle. Talk to other parents openly and honestly, without judgment.

You may feel at times like there is a conspiracy to get kids doing certain things (whether that is owning a smartphone or setting up an Instagram account) before you are ready for your child to take that step. You want to be able to go at your own pace, rather than feeling like an outlier or causing your child to feel left out.

If you want to build community with other parents focused on the challenges of raising kids in the digital age, you can start your own discussion group in person, on Facebook, or on another platform—it's really easy! Begin with a small circle of friends so it's manageable, and then you can expand later if you want. Send out an invitation, such as, "I am putting together an evening discussion around kids and technology, and I'd love for you to be part of the discussion." You'll be able to post questions to the group for everyone to see, or you can help answer questions from other members. I've found this strategy to be incredibly helpful, both as a parent and as someone who works with parents.

Wading into Social Media

For kids, social media is like a playground: everyone is talking at once and having a good time. To them, texting is analogous to a phone call, just easier and less obtrusive. Online games are like regular board games. You, as a parent, can approach this idea with judgment or you can see it for what it is, a parallel world. But this world still centers around making connections with other human beings.

Think of a portion of your kids' screen time this way: "they want to connect with their friends," rather than "they want to use their device." The device matters less than the motive. Your job is to look past the device and help them be a better friend, a better citizen, and a better person.

Rather than trying to learn everything all at once, try to learn one thing at a time. What is the most useful thing to learn about Snapchat or Instagram—right now? Maybe it's the privacy settings. Maybe it's how to set your profile picture. Don't get overwhelmed. Start with one thing and ramp up gradually.

It Takes a Village

If you feel completely ill equipped to dive into the social media or gaming sandbox with your child, you can try recruiting some help. Do you have a colleague or intern who is just out of college? This person might get you up to speed on the basics, so you get the fundamentals down. Or, do you have a niece who works in PR or social media, or a young friend of the family in high school or college who is a hard-core gamer? If your kid is all about Pinterest or Tumblr, do you have a niece or nephew who can mentor her? These friends and family can be excellent sources of information.

Depending on your comfort level, you may even be able to invite family or close friends into the sandbox with your child. For instance, if you give your thirteen-year-old permission to be on Instagram, you might let her know that her twenty-three-year-old cousin is there too—and following her because you asked her to. Of course, you may be on Instagram too, but that cousin is logging more hours and may be more clued in to the nuances!

Even if you can't get someone to hang out in social spaces with your kid, deputizing a chaperone can help. By asking a trusted adult to lightly watch your child's activities, you'll get some insight into what your child is "doing on there," which can be informative and reassuring at the same time.

Putting This into Practice

Get together with other parents to share what you know and what you need to learn. Don't get too focused on specific apps; instead, focus on experiences and categories of interaction, such as **content consumption** versus **content creation**. What is the attraction of a certain app for kids? What experiences have other parents' kids had that are negative, scary, or confusing with regard to their devices? Did something unexpected happen? Was there unplanned contact with a negative influence? Again, the app or device may be part of a bigger challenge—but instead of categorically rejecting the technology, we need to go deeper. Ask the parents of kids who are one or two years (or more) older than yours about their biggest surprises or rude awakenings in their kids' digital lives.

Finally, you can go straight to your kids and their friends and consult them as experts. Buy snacks and do a focus group. Have them tell you the best and the worst things about a particular game or a social app. Kids like to talk about their world. If they feel like you are genuinely interested, you should be able to get them to open up about it.

Now that you've assessed yourself and your beliefs about technology, let's reset. It's time to become a screenwise parent, someone who approaches technology not with fear but from a place of empowerment; someone who is comfortable with not knowing everything, and who will jump right in and learn; someone who is aware of the risks technology can bring, but is in control of the tools. It's time to become a parent who is ready to mentor young digital natives into fully realized digital citizens!

CHAPTER 4

Becoming a Tech-Positive Parent

Look around, and you might see technology invading our world rather than enhancing it. You're at a restaurant, and a family at another table is using technology to keep the kids quiet. You drop your fourth grader off at school and can't help but notice that some of the fifth and sixth graders, instead of playing or interacting, are standing alone or in small clumps looking intently at their phones with prematurely worried faces. Everyone seems to be avoiding each another.

How can we take advantage of the incredible opportunity offered by instant global communication to do something more important than finding out what our friends are wearing, what they are eating, and where they went on vacation? In this chapter, I'll offer some ways that you can lead your family toward positive uses of technology and boundaries that you feel good about. Screenwise uses of technology will engage your family with one another, encourage kids to move from screen- and tech-based activities into other interactions with the world, and improve their resourcefulness in the face of apps that don't do everything they want.

In their thoughtful book *The App Generation*, education

professor Howard Gardner and media scholar Katie Davis out-line the relationship with applications they observe in their current research on teenagers and young adults.[1] The transformative nature of life as mediated by apps is both unmistakable (think about check-ing documents for spelling and mapping a route) and subtle. Gard-ner and Davis describe two ways that kids can relate to the world via apps, and explain that we want our kids to be "app enabled" not "app dependent."[2] My perspective is that we should encourage kids to stretch beyond app-enabled life and use technology as a tool to solve problems.

You will be investing in your child's future when you help him learn not just how to use technology, but when to use it and what its best use is. A child who has used technology to support his goals and knows when to relate face to face and when to find other solu-tions will be well prepared for the challenges of life.

Digital citizenship is not just about technology, though—and that's where you come in. First, we need to make sure you're ready. You can't extract the rich potential from technology until you appre-ciate fully its positive aspect. You need to become a tech-positive parent.

What does a tech-positive parent look like?

- She creates a tech-positive environment, which can include planned, unplugged spaces and places.
- She thinks about her relationship with her own devices and recognizes that her behavior sets the tone for the whole family.
- He is a model of civility in his online and offline correspon-dence with friends, colleagues, his child's teacher, etc.
- She creates clearly defined boundaries and adheres to them, just as she expects other family members to adhere to them. Tech time doesn't interfere with unplugged time.

- He teaches and models respect for other people's boundaries in the digital world, asking permission before sharing or posting.
- He inspires a digital ethic that makes it feel wasteful to use the incredible gift of connectivity for navel-gazing, self-promotion, or obsessing about other people.
- She uses the power of technology to make a positive difference in the world.

Don't Assume the Worst

As a parent and mentor, it's up to you to set the tone and create the right environment for your kids, both offline and online. One of the best ways to do that is to start from the assumption that your children want to do the right thing; they just don't always know how. This simple assumption will open up many new ways to talk to kids about their world—about everything from their social interactions and games to their challenges and frustrations.

In my fieldwork, this overwhelmingly negative feeling that many parents and educators have about kids "abusing" technology comes up over and over again, which is why I think of it as one of the most damaging barriers to tech-positive parenting. Open channels of communication are key to a healthy relationship with your child, and the doors slam shut when we start by assuming bad intentions on the child's part. Even a mild assumption that kids are just "wasting time" with technology makes it difficult to have an open conversation.

Parents and educators always get much further with young people when they assume the best. Kids' intentions are usually pretty basic and innocent—they simply want to connect with friends, find like-minded peers, and communicate their identities and feelings. Technology can add layers of complexity to these natural desires, but that's why they need your guidance. And as strange as it may sound, they often *want* your help.

Framing the Discussion

Creating and facilitating learning networks infused with the values of positive speech and kindness has a huge effect on our kids. The world of social media may seem foreign to those who are not digital natives, but it's really very like the real world. If you teach kids to participate in their digital world in a positive and engaged way, the effects will carry over to their interactions at home, in school, and beyond.

As a rule, you want to make sure nothing will take away people's positive impressions. Telling your child, "You are a good person and a great friend—and you want your posts to reflect that," is much better than saying, "You are being mean." If you are trying to correct a serious issue and this more optimistic approach doesn't work, then it may be time to be more directly critical. You'll have to make that call based on the situation, but starting with praise for the desired behavior is generally a lot more effective than criticizing the misstep.

Helping Kids Get Screenwise

There are great teaching opportunities all around you, in the very networks your kids inhabit. A great way to foster discernment in your kids is to have your children learn to make their own critical assessments of the media they use. Have your kids show you other kids' digital profiles—and have them identify the ones they think are positive and point out others that are less so. Have them make the determination, and avoid "filling in the blanks" for them.

Your kids are not the only ones who will benefit from this assessment. You will, too. This exercise offers you excellent insight into their standards, and gives you a great starting point as a mentor. You'll get to see their values, their opinions, and their criteria for judgment. From my interviews with seventh graders, I can tell you that kids are often highly judgmental of other kids.

Of course, we want kids to have standards for what they would and would not share, but we also need to be wary of their judgment being too harsh. We obviously don't want our children inflicting harm or calling other kids negative names. There's a balance here: we want to teach them judgment, but we also want to help them be less judgmental. As parents, we should never judge kids' photos in mean-spirited ways. You may think, "He looks like he's trying to be a thug," in that picture, but it's better to say, "What impression do you think he's going for?," and let your child discern for himself how that's working out. You can certainly say that it isn't a good decision to be sharing pictures like that, but don't make any judgments about a child's character (or his parents' character) to your child. Instead, talk through the pitfalls of self-representation in a sympathetic way that helps clarify boundaries. For example, you could respond, "Sometimes people feel like they need a *lot* of attention and response to a picture, and that feeling might make it challenging to make smart choices."

Consequences Can Be a Clue

In some cases, kids themselves can decide what the negative consequences of a digital misstep should be. Sometimes the experience itself may offer its own consequence. For example, friends may get mad when one friend shares something that the others feel offended by. Parents may not need to add consequences; mentoring your child about how to make up with her friends may be more helpful in that situation.

When a school brought me in to consult after a fifth-grade relationship misstep involving a planned exchange of naked pictures (yes, it can happen that young!), the school was considering suspending all the students who forwarded the image. In that incident, the public embarrassment the originator of the photo suffered was likely more than enough punishment for that particular eleven-year-old. Instead of punishing students, schools can mentor kids with a focus on teaching them not to forward such images, especially without clear consent of the subject. For the peers who mean-spiritedly forwarded the image, a consequence of some kind may have been appropriate, but even for these kids, some reflective education and guided mentorship offer the best chance of behavioral change.

How can you talk to your kids about the potential consequences of mistakes and prepare them for these issues as they arise? Focus on the fact that your child wants to be a good friend and to be perceived that way. Ask your child: What does a nice person or good friend do? If you are a teacher or a school administrator and all your policies sound like you are policing the kids and assuming they will do the worst, how does that feel? How does it feel when your company monitors your e-mail, for instance? Ideally, schools and parents should frame the rules in positive ways.

Thinking Beyond Screen Time

When we label all technology use as "screen time," we fail to make a crucial distinction between creativity and consumption. Truly, technology use exists on a continuum. For example, watching a TV show is consuming passively, but what about watching a YouTube video about how to play Minecraft? What about *making* a YouTube video about how to play Minecraft? What about a Tumblr blog with mostly reposted content—a scrapbook or collage, if you will. What about a Tumblr blog (or any blog, really) populated with original content? These are all hues in the rainbow of engagement.

For many of us, social media is an exercise in (mostly) consumption—we view pictures, videos, and other links that our friends and family have shared. But for others, social media is a creative outlet. It's a chance to make things, to show off creativity, to get feedback, and to share and learn. These are valuable experiences that are no different from similar activities in the analog world.

Not all screen time is created equal. So let's think differently about screen time limits—at least let's move away from absolute, hard-and-fast time limits. For instance, is your kid is composing a song using GarageBand, or is she binge watching a Netflix series? Binge watching can have its place (if you have a cold, or if you make it a family activity), but I would set different time limits for these two very different activities.

One way to help your kids make the transition from consuming to creating is to suggest that they create a parody of their favorite (or least favorite) show. Or you can encourage them to craft their own book using Book Creator, or produce their own show using simple video editing software.

Share with your kids the idea of belonging and contributing to a community. Shared communities exist for everything you can think of, including knitting, cooking Greek food, playing Minecraft, etc. What can you contribute to a community? As a mentor, you can model the idea of healthy participation in a digital—or real-world—community. That's digital citizenship!

Setting Kids Up for Success

How can you push your child to take advantage of the vast possibilities of the Internet? It's up to us as parents and mentors to introduce opportunities to engage in meaningful ways. Show your child a newspaper from another country, or suggest that everyone in the family find a newspaper article that represents a perspective different from his own. Reading something you disagree with is a great way to learn empathy and respect for others' perspectives. Let your child know that being exposed to other ideas doesn't mean that you have to change your mind—that's not the point. With this activity, you'll be giving your child a window into another opinion, which can be valuable in helping him form his own opinions.

Another idea is to have your family research an upcoming family vacation together. A fourth grader can look into museums or nature hikes near your potential destination, or a sixth grader could calculate the mileage and create a budget for gas needed on the road trip. Everyone in the family might enjoy charting the course between point A and point B, and finding fun places to stop along the way. Maybe your child would like to create a blog, Tumblr, or social media stream dedicated to the trip.

The Power of Authentic Audiences

One of the exciting things about the way technology enables sharing is that our work can reach more authentic audiences. That audience does not have to be huge—in fact, it can be quite small. The important thing is that it is interested in our project or our process.

Such creative endeavors are much more than mindless pursuits. Maybe your daughter is learning to write and is honing her craft in a digital space with a small but eager and receptive audience. What a terrific way to learn to write! Perhaps you have a blog or Tumblr about adoption or recipes you've created. Maybe only twelve people read it, but they care about it. Producing content for an audience is a different experience from writing an assignment in English class. For our kids, writing papers that only the teacher reads is far less engaging than creating content that they can share with classmates and others. By high school, if not sooner, kids' work can be part of a public digital portfolio.

Encourage Collaboration

Creating parts of a whole can be a great exercise for your children. One of the huge advantages of digital creations is that the tools promote collaboration—but how can your family use such collaboration tools? You may already be working collaboratively at your office—why not at home too? You'll be teaching critical skills to your children.

A simple way to start is by creating a shared Google calendar. Soccer practice, playdates, fund-raisers, rehearsals for the school play—sometimes it seems like all we're doing is running from one activity to another. A shared calendar can teach responsibility, accountability, and time management. You may not want to give your child editing privileges on a shared calendar right away—but working together to create a viable schedule is a very good skill. A high school student can (and probably should!) be maintaining his own calendar.

Getting More Out of Games

Games are a powerful way for families to come together. Traditional board games are a time-honored tradition, but interactive digital games have the potential to be just as powerful as their analog counterparts. To keep kids engaged and excited, consider designating a family game night once a week, alternating unplugged and "plugged in" games each time. Let your child introduce you to her favorite game and see what you like. Cut the Rope, Agar.io, or Minecraft might be far more fun than you anticipated.

Opportunities for creativity abound. Urge your kids to design their own game, or to improve the ones they have. For kids who aren't ready for actual video game design, prototype the action with pen and paper. This is a great way to get them thinking about how to improve day-to-day life using technology. Have them iterate different versions of their favorite application or game.

Ask your kids to show you how to play the games they like, and play with them sometimes. There's a hidden benefit for parents in such collaborative gaming: participating with your kids in their games—and watching them interact with others—gives you a great window into their world. You get to experience it yourself. Of course, this requires that you take the time to learn enough about your kids' interests that you can engage in the games they are passionate about. In my experience working with parents, it's worth the time investment. There's simply no substitute for the insight you can gather as a participant.

If your kids took up chess or lacrosse and you did not know how to play, you might learn more about these games so you could understand their experiences. Digital games are the same—so get in there and play Minecraft! Try out "survival mode" for basics and "creative mode" if you want to see the digital worlds other kids are creating. Play with your kids sometimes, and watch them. Know what is at stake in their gaming world.

It is also important to understand some of the benefits of interactive games. Kids can learn to work out conflict, assess the strengths of a team, and divide labor. In some games, kids allocate roles based on particular players' strengths. If you play Clash of Clans together, what does it mean to be in a clan with your kids?

Of course, kids playing interactive games with strangers can lead to challenges, and this is the biggest source of fear for most parents. Ideally, kids aged twelve and under should be playing with people they know. Some schools or groups of families have set up individual Minecraft servers so that kids can play together without parents having to worry that their children are interacting with unknown adults. If you want to set up such a server and need help, reach out to the IT person at your child's school (or even at a local college) to see if she can recommend a high school or college student who might be able to help you. It's not difficult to set up a private server, and the peace of mind it brings may be worth the effort.

Sometimes the dynamics of game play bleed into other interactions, too. Classroom teachers have told me that children have expanded their social circles by playing games like Minecraft with kids they didn't previously relate to. For some children, gaming has opened up new avenues for making friends, a positive thing.

On the other hand, fourth-, fifth-, and sixth-grade teachers have shared with me stories about conflicts that have arisen in games, which can make their way into class time and sometimes continue throughout the day. While upper elementary school students can and should learn to settle interpersonal disputes on their own, it is important that you stay in touch with your child's teacher if conflicts surrounding online games have been coming up during the school day. You want to support your child's interaction within a community, especially when it affects another sphere, like school.

One teacher described a meeting with parents of her avid Minecrafters at which some parents were incensed that they had been called in, as they considered gaming a part of their children's private lives. If you are a parent in such a situation, try to be gracious to the teacher, as she is likely seeing an opportunity for social mentorship that does not come up during class hours. Also remember that, even if your child is thriving, there may be a more vulnerable kid in the mix who needs help.

Talking to Young Players

Two fifth-grade boys, Jonathan and Elliot, spent an afternoon with me explaining their relationship to Minecraft and other games that are played on a public server. One of the kids was busy building (in Minecraft) parks and buildings in his neighborhood. The boys' extensive familiarity with the options and different modes for play is impressive. A game in which you have so much control over designing the "world" where you are playing is appealing to both children and adults.

Both of these boys and their parents feel that gaming integrates pretty well into the mix of friendship, homework, family life, and sleep. Elliot's mother clarifies that time to play is dependent on Elliot's completion of other obligations; he must have finished his homework and taken care of his chores and responsibilities at home before he can play. What strikes me most is the boys' pride in their accumulated knowledge and skill as well as their camaraderie in playing together.

Criteria for Choosing Apps

Marina Umaschi Bers is a Tufts professor and games researcher (check out her fabulous TEDx talk!).[3] I particularly love Bers's concept of "playgrounds versus playpens." I find myself using this metaphor when I make my own decisions about choosing applications and experiences I want to share with my son, and I am drawn to applications that foster creativity and have more open-ended possibilities. Bers points out, and I agree, that many playpen-type experiences (think flashcard apps) are harmless, but they do not offer children a chance to grow by taking risks and increasing autonomy and mastery.[4]

Educators (and many parents, too!) are excited to see children learning coding, with good reason. There are plenty of guided lessons in resources like Scratch (specifically for young kids) and Codecademy, and learning how to write simple code gives kids a blank slate to create and explore. Bers shows that "coding is the new literacy" and argues that we should start STEM (science, technology, engineering, and math) education while kids are still young, before they've internalized stereotypes about what kinds of kids are "good" or "not good" at STEM fields.

Playpens are meant to restrict children to a small area or defined set of activities—they limit risks, but they also limit learning. The digital media environment, especially in games like LittleBigPlanet or Minecraft, is more like a playground. There may be opportunities to collaborate, which isn't always easy. In games like those mentioned, kids design their own world and make decisions about how to play. Like real playgrounds, digital playgrounds entail some risk—including frustration, disappointment, and negative interactions with other kids. But they also offer positive challenges and the potential for learning!

Allowing your kids to visit the digital playground requires that you give up a little control, but I find that the rewards are worth it. Here's how to apply this metaphor to apps and media content:

- Choose applications that encourage your child to connect with others.
- Consider games that encourage cooperation and collaboration in problem solving.
- Find games that encourage kids to create, not just play. There are many games that let kids create and customize characters, levels, or environments.
- As much as possible, look for empathy-building games.
- Try to find games that don't oversexualize female characters and avatars.

How can you find such games? For one, ask slightly older kids what the best games are—and why. I find that sixth graders have strong opinions about why a game might or might not be good for second graders! Also check blogs such as Cool Mom Tech, Amy Kraft's *Media Macaroni*, and *Geek Dad*. For Minecraft videos with no inappropriate language, check out this great site, curated by kids: Clean Minecraft Videos (cleanminecraftvideos.com).

How Much Do You Want to Limit?

Simply put, games are fun. Kids can get caught up in the immersive world of a game and its social interaction. The allure is so great that they'll often get obsessed or "addicted" to a game. Or they'll suspend good judgment because they are so immersed. Understandably, this can cause family friction.

There are two types of limits: time limits and content limits. We already talked about screen time limits, but what should you do when you feel that the content of a particular app or game is inappropriate for your child? I see parents instinctively try to apply controls using the device itself, by setting up passcodes or installing "nanny apps." While some mobile devices can be set up to restrict content, don't overrely on these automated controls. They are blunt instruments that are not foolproof—and they might also block some great content.

Instead of blocking the things that worry you, engage your kids in creative thinking and social critique about games. Take, for example, Grand Theft Auto. Ask your kids why they think it is okay to play a game about stealing cars. Or, you can start from a position that you recognize that they know stealing cars is bad, but sometimes it is fun to playact things we would never do. These are important conversations to have with your kids.

Try to understand the pleasures and challenges inherent in different games. What you are really trying to do is minimize the struggles over limits. When you understand your children's motivations—and they understand your perspective—you'll be in a better position to manage limits without a battle.

Taste and Choices

If my mother didn't like something I liked, she'd say I had "taste in my toenails." Given the many hours I spent watching terrible TV shows, I can't blame her judgment. As parents, we can attempt to influence our sons' and daughters' tastes in media, books, music, or food—but ultimately, we can't control their tastes. Here are some pragmatic ways to stretch past "PBJ and pizza" media and cultivate your kids' critical thinking skills without undermining their choices and/or insulting what they like.

Your best chance to influence your kids comes when they are young. Did you love *The Muppet Movie*? They probably will too. Like the Beatles? Johnny Cash? Madonna? This is your chance to initiate your child. Use Netflix, iTunes, and YouTube to introduce your kids to the amazing media of our past. When Pete Seeger died, our son was devastated, and he was a little shocked that his classmates didn't know who Pete Seeger was. Successful indoctrination at home!

It can take a lot of work to keep up with the latest kids' TV shows, applications, and games. Let someone else do it for you! Follow bloggers who critically evaluate apps, shows, and games for kids. Two I love are Media Macaroni (mediamacaroni.com) and Geek-Dad (geekdad.com), but there are dozens of other great ones. Maybe you can even start your own blog based on what you learn!

Use social media to check in with your community about the best and worst apps out there. There is a lot of junk, unfortunately—but there are also some true gems.

Opportunities for Kids with Social Challenges

For all the complexities of social media, such platforms can actually offer some help to kids with special needs and/or social challenges. Socially isolated kids can find one another online in communities of shared interest. They can make connections that might be more difficult if attempted in person. The asynchronous and performative nature of social media can give kids more time to present themselves without awkwardness, and this can be a huge confidence boom to kids who may struggle to fit in with peers. Through social media and other digital tools you can:

- Share your experiences and network with other parents and families.
- Use Meetup (or similar spaces) to help kids with niche interests find a community of shared interests, such as games, hobbies, crafts, etc. Be sure to accompany kids to any in-person meet up, of course—and maybe even online ones, especially if the kids are young.
- Look for apps for kids with special needs. One that may work for families with—or without—special needs is the highly customizable app Choiceworks, which helps kids check items off a list. Some kids love swiping completed tasks off the list. If you have a dawdler or are working on independent self-care, this app could be very helpful.
- Ask your child's teachers to take some pictures, videos, or audio recordings of the day's activities. They may or may not choose to do it, but it is one way you can find out more about your child's world—especially if you have a child who is not very verbal.

Social media presents some special considerations for parents of children with special needs. For example, disclosing your child's diagnosis on social media might seem like a fine way to get support for the challenges you experience when she is three years old, but your daughter may not appreciate such openness when she's twenty and interviewing for a job.

Are You a Screenwise Parent Yet?

I hope that this chapter has helped you reset your perspective. Maybe you were already a tech-positive parent, and the information in this chapter just affirms your position. Or perhaps you were anxious about your kids' immersion in all things tech, yet you want to understand their world. Embracing a new outlook on digital interactions takes time. You can't be expected to make wholesale changes all at once. Take small steps every day to adjust your mindset. You'll have an easier time empathizing with your kids and gain a deeper understanding of their digital world.

Ask yourself the following questions to do a tech-positive self-assessment:

- Do you foster a tech-positive environment in your home?
- Do you see the Internet as a huge positive, provided it's used the right way?
- Do you employ empathy and avoid rushing to judgment about your kids' tech use?
- Do you model responsible device use for your family?
- Do you offer opportunities for creativity with technology?
- Do you play some of the same digital games as your kids?
- Do the tech rules in your house apply to you as well as to your kids?
- Do you set clear boundaries about tech time and unplugged time?
- Have you reduced (or eliminated) battles over tech time limits and content restrictions?
- Do you ask your child's permission before posting pictures of her?

- Can you demonstrate—and even defend—the true potential of connectivity?

- Ultimately, are you using technology to make a positive difference in the world?

Now that you've assessed your own digital literacy, it's time to start putting your knowledge into practice.

CHAPTER 5

Empathy Is the App

Now that you are a tech-positive parent, you're ready to get started on your path to becoming a media mentor. But what does this look like in practice? How can you stay true to your own values and allay your concerns while supporting your child?

In this chapter, I will address ways you can use your own curiosity and wisdom to arrive at a place of empathy for your child—and other children—growing up in our always-on, always-connected world. This is not about simply letting your kid do whatever she wants; instead, I want to help you make decisions that make sense for your family from a perspective that is connected rather than judgmental.

Curiosity Is the Key to Understanding

First, let's get *curious*. Think about your child, or each child in your family, and all the things that she is supposed to do on any given day (or week). Consider her school day, homework, after-school activities, extended family time, chores, the religious or social

communities she is involved with, and anything she needs to practice (musical instrument, gymnastics, etc.). Then think about how
devices and connectivity filter in and out throughout the day.

In a quick assessment, what do you see? Is your child online early
in the morning before you wake up? Does she check her texts the
second she walks out of school? Does she call you from her phone
and talk to you as she walks home from school? Think about the
purpose of these moments. Is texting a way to connect with friends
she doesn't get to see? Is watching a TV show her way of relaxing? Sometimes, these moments don't yield the results our kids are
seeking. The same holds true for adults who use social media as
downtime—it is not always so relaxing.

Another question to ask: Does the activity your child wants to
do have such a strong pull that it would be on the top of his list at
any time? For instance, is a social app or an online game so capti-
vating that your kid seems obsessed with it? Is it frustrating? Ultimately, you want understand your child's motivations, to get really
curious about his world. This will put you in a much better position
to mentor your child.

Motivations and Environments

Just like your own life, your kid's life is full of social and physical
stresses. Some kids have a harder time coping with these than other
kids do. And stress looks different on each kid. For instance, if you
know your child never gets to finish his lunch during his too-short
lunch break, then you know he is arriving home or at his after-care
program hungry and depleted. Older kids who are more self-aware
may recognize this, but younger kids may not know that they are hungry or tired or need help, which can lead them to make bad decisions.

When you are starving, a huge, unhealthy snack may be appealing. And, as in the real world, it is hard to make positive choices about digital activities when you are feeling depleted.

When you review the week in relation to your child's tech use, you may find things that make you cringe. Maybe you are okay with Minecraft but you dislike your daughter's YouTube habit. Maybe you like your son's study group on Google Hangouts but you can't stand his favorite Netflix show.

Be honest with yourself about your concerns. Let's say that your daughter is starting to get attention from boys and she seems excited and nervous. Would she acquiesce to a boy's request for a revealing picture? Would she send one, thinking it is a good way to flirt? Don't assume the worst, but don't believe that a serious incident could never happen. Many kids will try things when they are alone with their devices that they would never do when someone else was in the room with them.

There are plenty of examples of kids making impulsive choices. Stories about high school sexting scandals, in which nearly every student in a high school community has nude pictures on their phones, have become common. For example, widespread sharing of nude and sexual images among high school students in Canon City, Colorado, became mainstream news.[1] When interviewed, students in Canon suggested that sharing nude pictures of themselves and other students was a common practice. Pause for a second before reacting. Instead of getting disgusted, try to imagine going to high school today. Other kids are sending naked pictures as part of their flirting and dating rituals. Are you sure you wouldn't have tried it?

It is perfectly okay to have a strong response! And of course, it is okay to limit or forbid things, too. You're the parent, after all. But try to understand what motivates kids. Your ability to mentor is stronger if you understand the *reasons* kids do things.

How You Can Model Empathy

Empathy has to start with you. As parents, we should have far more empathy for ourselves than we often do—and we need to empathize more with our co-parents, as well as with other parents. It is really hard to raise kids in this crazy world. We are quick to judge ourselves and other parents, whether it is a mom on her iPhone at the playground instead of gazing into her child's eyes with adoration, a dad who gets his kid a device at an age we wouldn't choose, or a father who sends his kid with a lunch we'd never pack. We need to have empathy for the context of their choices. That parent may have a sick family member or a work crisis going on. That parent may be on the phone with the child's social worker. You don't always know what's going on with other people. And you may not be giving yourself credit for what's going on with you. As my own family has weathered stressful moves, school changes, financial stress, and job changes, things at home may not be as robust as they are when we are feeling more stable. Be the best parent you can be on that day, and know that on another day you may well do better, but you are always doing your best. So think about all the different directions we need to send our empathy. We need to cultivate:

- Empathy for other parents
- Empathy for kids
- Empathy for teachers
- Empathy for ourselves—it is hard to be a parent!

We model empathy for our kids' teachers when we remind our children not to burden teachers with unnecessary communication in their off hours. If your child didn't write down the homework assignment, she can get it from a friend.

Finally, remember how hard it can be for your kids to deal with the constant pressure to be connected, the endless ability to compare—their vacation, their birthday party, even their family—with what other kids are posting. By acknowledging that you get it, you are aligning yourself with your child and positioning yourself as a trusted mentor.

Finding Opportunities to Model Good Behavior

When we were kids, so many means of communication were public or semipublic. For instance, we heard our parents or siblings on the central home phone, and we heard strangers on pay phones. We learned the proper way to answer the phone and how to end a phone conversation politely, too. From these interactions, we also learned when *not* to make—or receive—a call. We learned who had communication priority and we had time limits on our calls so we wouldn't create a busy signal for someone trying to reach our parents or siblings. Some of these rules were explained explicitly, while others we simply absorbed.

Now, because we all carry our own phone or tablet, we have to seek opportunities to model a thoughtful approach to using them. Today, many of our digital interactions are private, especially when we use personal devices. In other words, it's extremely difficult for kids to glean behavioral cues when activities are not as "public."

Even as parents get frustrated about how public children's digital lives seem to be, they are often at least as concerned about how private they are. Having individual devices makes the moment of sharing very private, and can make us forget that we are putting our innermost thoughts into a "stream" of information that is—or can be—shared with others.

Think back to when we were children. When our friends called, our parents might answer the phone. We could overhear others and be overheard ourselves. Today's children are getting their own communication devices in early elementary school, in some cases. Many kids have smartphones by fifth grade. The devices and rules have changed, for sure, but that shouldn't mean anarchy. If anything, we need to be more explicit in our teaching, because so much communication is individual to individual. You have to be proactive; simple demonstration and modeling don't happen on their own.

The next chapter is all about family life, but here are some simple ways to mentor your children in digital communication etiquette:

- Consider letting your children see how and when you use text messages to communicate. Obviously, you'll want to keep certain text messages private, but sharing some texts is a great opportunity to model communication for them.
- Talk to your kids about oversharing. Not just the dangerous or explicit stuff, but the boring stuff too! Show them how we sometimes find certain kinds of posts tiresome, and might even unfollow someone because of them.
- Show them an example of "slacktivism" on Facebook (when people post their political opinions and memes but don't do very much to effect change on these issues in the real world). If we feel strongly about a topic or a cause and we post about it, what else are we doing about that topic? If something is truly important, it should be reflected in our offline behaviors too.

Every Day Is Picture Day

Remember picture day at school? I hated picture day. There was a permanence to it that was terrifying. I knew my parents would have that wallet-sized photo of me forever, so I felt like I had one shot to get it right. Smile right, wear the right clothes, and make sure your eyes were open, for heaven's sake! For today's kids, every day is picture day.

One facet of our kids' lives that we need to get curious about is what it is like to be constantly photographed. Most of us take pictures of our kids on a regular basis, whereas when we were children, cameras only came out on special occasions in most families. Do you wish there were more pictures of you as a tween? Probably not. Think about your top ten most embarrassing moments as a tween and imagine that there were pictures to record each of your failings.

By middle school, armed with smartphones, kids and their friends are taking pictures constantly. At any time, someone can snap a picture of your child: asleep on the school bus on the way home from a class trip, possibly drooling a little; in the locker room changing; or at any number of other inopportune moments.

Also, photos mean something different to our kids than they did to us. Today, we live in a more visual culture. Cameras are everywhere, built into the devices we carry with us at all times. Digital photos cost nothing to take, nothing to store, and nothing to share. Your child's experiences of seeing a photo right away and judging whether it is good or bad ("No, don't send this one to Dad; send this one!") are part of his growing up. As your child enters different stages of social awareness and self-consciousness, and as his peers start taking pictures, his experience of photos—which ones he likes and wants to share and which he wants deleted—will change in meaning once again.

Having a photo mark every experience is an expectation for today's kids, but the proliferation of images also lowers the impact of each photo in our kids' minds. We fret over our child's "permanent" record but don't spend enough time thinking about the permanence and publicity when we use our social media wall as a family album.

The Power of Asking Permission

Are you contributing to the problem of proliferating photos? Are you snapping pictures constantly, recording each mini-milestone? It's tempting, isn't it? The urge is the same as it ever was, to preserve our kids' precious childhood in some way. But because photos are a way to communicate, they can add a hidden layer of complexity.

As a proud parent, you may think that you are innocently sharing images. Your kids may take it in an entirely different way. What you think is cute might be devastating to them. It's easy to fall into this trap, but empathy can help. Here's what I always recommend, and this step can make a huge positive culture shift in your family: start asking permission to share photos. Yes, ask your child permission. Your request sends a message, and will accomplish some important things:

• It teaches your child that her image is her own. It helps her recognize that sharing is a choice and that some things are private. Because you showed her that consideration and modeled some respect for her privacy, she'll be more likely to ask before she shares a picture of her friend.

- It teaches good boundaries. It's important for a child to know that she can say no. The very act of asking for permission creates a moment for her to stop and think. This pause is very helpful: we could all benefit from it.

- It teaches empowerment. Asking permission bestows power on your child. Posting a photo is now her choice, not yours. It's a wonderful gift, and she'll start to expect the same consideration from her friends. Your daughter will feel empowered to say, "Don't share that," when someone takes a photo of her. She can insist, "Show me that you are erasing that."

- It teaches self-control. Now that you've established the guidelines of respect, urge your child to ask herself for permission to take or share a "selfie." Social media is part of journaling, recording feelings, and celebrating small moments. You don't want to quash that, but you want her to think about the ramifications.

Asking your child for permission before sharing photos of her creates a respectful relationship. Your child will have a better understanding of this complex social exchange because you've modeled it. It will help her understand why it's important, too. Talk to your child about how your respect for her makes her feel, and urge her to think about how others feel when she's the one taking the photo of her friends.

By respecting your children's wishes, you are modeling the basics of healthy relationships. This will pay dividends beyond photo sharing: it will form a good foundation for your child to make better decisions when navigating the new participatory media landscape.

Mentoring over Monitoring

Parenting is difficult. While we may try to optimize other parts of
our life, parenting doesn't seem to offer many such opportunities.
There are no shortcuts.

For instance, it can be tempting to install software that will let
you know and/or control everything your child does online. You
might think you've "solved" the issue with content blockers or apps
that impose time limits. But unfortunately, you can't let technology
do the work of parenting for you.

This is why I'm such a strong proponent of mentoring over monitoring. Not only is mentoring more effective when it comes to technology issues, but also it puts your kids in a better position to make
sound decisions in their offline world too. The values you teach
them about online communication are the values that are important
to you and your family.

Some of the biggest questions I get from the parents with whom I
work are about balance. One question is, "How do you stay involved
without being too overbearing?" You want to insert yourself into
your kids' digital world, but if you push too hard you're "out." You
also may wish to use some monitoring as a part of your parenting
toolkit. The question is, "If I'm going to monitor my kids' online
activities, how do I do it the right way?" Some monitoring may help
you mentor. And some is unhelpful.

With hundreds of "nanny apps" like Net Nanny available,
should we be spying on our kids? As with any tool, the way you use
it is important. If an app is your only tool for managing your child's
digital world, it will fail you. But using such apps in conjunction
with mentoring can be effective.

If you intend to monitor your kids, I strongly suggest you that you let them know in advance. First of all, no one likes surprises after the fact. Your monitoring will feel like a violation to your child—because it is. Plus, their knowledge that they are being monitored gives them a chance to choose their actions. In other words, you give them control, even though you are watching.

It's important to let kids know why you are checking on their digital activities. Let them know that your monitoring is not about their behavior, but that you are concerned about potential dangers they may not have considered. Plus, you'd prefer they do the right thing; you don't actually want to "catch" them doing the wrong thing, so you want to give them every opportunity to show good behavior.

We do need to mentor our kids. And we need to think about the benefits and the downsides of spying. If you have the kind of relationship with your kid that leads you to consider covert spying, he may be on to you already. A few kids do go to great lengths to hide their online activities (for example, posting to a family-friendly Instagram account but also to another "private" one, or using a fake name), but, for the most part, if your child is engaging with others on his accounts those are probably his "real" profiles.

When people do "spy" on their kids, the things they learn, and their children's responses, vary. One blog post by a father who followed his child's activities using surveillance worthy of the NSA brought a strong (mostly negative) response from online commenters.[2] The father tracked his daughter extensively, and the results were surprising. For instance, he learned that his daughter was very interested in writing fan fiction and spent many hours perfecting her work. He was proud of her writing and felt that his increased knowledge of his daughter's hobbies, as well as a single mention of drug use at a party, justified the snooping. The comments on the father's post were mostly negative, and pointed out that kids need spaces to talk about ideas (atheism and veganism were brought up by different commenters) and identities (homosexuality was brought up by another commenter).

One commenter was especially vehement in his criticism of the author: "There's a difference between monitoring your children and seriously invading your children's privacy.... Rather than be amazed that your daughter has a hobby of writing fiction, something you found out from invading her privacy, you should be more curious as to why she didn't choose to reveal that to you."[3]

Much of what this commenter says resonates with me. We want to know our children, and that includes letting them choose to tell us about certain aspects of their lives. Or not. Letting our kids know we are there for them and that we have rules about their online life is different from reading every word they post.

Another example of the challenging issues that spying brings up is mentioned in the great book *This Is a Book for Parents of Gay Kids*. The book wisely suggests giving kids a chance to come out to parents on their own timeline and not using tech snooping to "catch" the child. Instead, the authors focus on what you can do to create a safe environment so that a child who is gay or questioning might be more comfortable sharing with you.[4]

Monitoring Kids' Texting

We parents need to understand what texting is for, and must be able to guide our kids without depending on tech-enabled spying. If we consider texting more like phone calls, we may wish to supervise. I would suggest that proper use of e-mail and phone calls—though both are of limited interest to our children—are still skills that need to be taught. Listening in to kids' calls or having a look at their incoming and outgoing e-mails, with their knowledge, when they are still in the training wheels phase is a great idea.

To kids, texting is like hanging out with friends—the kind of hanging out you may have done with little supervision when you were a child. My husband walked to kindergarten on his own in the 1970s. How many kindergartners walk to school on their own today? Norms about supervision have shifted dramatically, and our kids have fewer and fewer chances to play together and interact outside of organized activities or supervised playdates or get-togethers. Texting and social media fill some of that casual hanging out role.

One challenge for our kids is digital permanence—the fact that the message they send to a friend can be shared, taken out of context, or even kept for reexamination. This is very different from words spoken face to face, where facial cues can signal misunderstandings and issues can be more quickly settled. Texting has its own etiquette, which is still evolving—rapidly, at that.

What Are You Looking For?

My first question to parents who do choose to read their child's texts is, "What are you looking for?" What do you hope to see? Before we try to catch our kids doing the wrong thing, we need to think about whether we have done a good enough job modeling the right things. Have we thought enough about what we want them to do, compared with the amount of thinking we do about catching them doing the wrong thing?

We worry too much about salacious news headlines and not enough about the kind of people our children will become. Will they be thoughtful in their communication? And will they take advantage of the incredible power of digital sharing to create positive outcomes?

Most parents' fears about their kids' digital activities turn out to be unfounded. For the most part, what you find when you look at kids' texts is that they are very, very boring.

We need to get curious about kids' lived experiences with technology in order to help them navigate the pressures of performing and making their lives look a certain way. You've seen it, I'm sure: on Facebook, everyone's life is presented in its most idealized form. As adults, we know that's not reality. But do our kids understand that? Also, for teens and tweens, how do the issues of digital footprints constrain young people at a time when they should be able to experiment with their identities? Just because they're going through a phase (fascinated by a certain kind of music, art, or hobby, for example) doesn't mean that it should be associated with them permanently.

Media scholar Danah Boyd suggests that the more ephemeral apps, where photos either disappear (Snapchat) or get buried in a busy feed (Instagram), might be more attractive to young people than Facebook, with its photo album feel and easy-to-search archives. Indeed, I enjoy my "year in review" on Facebook in part because I am an adult. I've got the same friends and hairstyle and tastes that I did a year ago, so the year in review is a pleasant experience, not a reminder of an identity I'd like to distance myself from.

If You Do Monitor

Once you've told your children that you will be monitoring them, the next step is to assess what you will do with the information you learn. Before reading their texts, you may want to think about what your response will be to:

- Bad language
- Negative talk about other kids

- Negative talk about adults/teachers
- Negative talk about you or other parents

Ask yourself whether you will see your children's friends differently if you are reading their private conversations. What did you talk about with your friends at their age? What would be a yellow flag to you? What would be a red flag? Have you advised them what to do if they get a message that makes them uncomfortable, such as an inappropriate picture, mean words about a classmate, or an accusation or threat? Make sure they know that they can come to you in this situation—and that they won't be in trouble.

If you are reading kids' communication and see things other kids are saying that you don't like, or that your own kid is doing, tread carefully. You may want to ask some open-ended questions about what's going on rather than confronting your child directly. Try "How are you feeling about things between you and Sean?" instead of "Sean is such a jerk to you and I can't stand the language he uses to text you."

If your child is having trouble, you may want to place some new limits, but be careful with this. Overreacting may put him into "covert operations" mode and drive him to be sneaky. If you notice that negative things seem to be happening late at night, you could certainly set a limit that smartphones and tablets need to be put away (or placed in the parents' room) at night. You can disable Wi-Fi, but if your child uses a cellular network, that won't have much effect.

If you have reason to believe your child is being bullied, is in an abusive relationship, or is getting inappropriate or threatening texts from a peer (or an adult), of course you should take action. But if we are talking about the everyday social dramas of elementary, middle, and even high school, you can be more helpful by offering support than by being overbearing.

Last, what are the consequences for a misstep on your child's part? Will you take away texting or phone privileges? Will you allow "natural consequences" (for example, her friends getting mad or her homework not getting done) to run their course? If your child orders or downloads an app without permission, can you lay out a different process, perhaps greenlighting the app if she meets certain conditions? While you can't know what will happen in advance, it helps to think these issues through before you get started.

Alternatives to Spying

If you've been doing some good mentoring around your children's digital activities, you may find that the training wheels can come off. Perhaps you can do this little by little. Use a "gradient" of sorts to wean your kids—and yourself—from monitoring. The milestones are very personal, and will depend on mutual trust.

A simple gradient is time. For instance, suppose you started with a rule that there would be no texting with friends after 7 p.m. Changing the time to 8 p.m. is a good next step. It may be a small difference, but it's a show of trust. You can make such changes with the understanding that they can be revoked if the rules are abused. Maybe the next step is 9 p.m. It sounds like an insignificant change, but it could mean a lot to your child. Now he can text with his friend about the basketball game he's watching.

If you feel that establishing specific rules is too intrusive, consider just letting kids know that in their first year of texting you plan to drop in periodically—and unexpectedly—to make sure their communication is appropriate. This approach tells them you'll be watching, but that you generally trust them. Just be clear up front about what you consider to be appropriate. Again, your goal is to teach them, not to "catch" them.

Another tactic is letting them show you what they are doing, instead of "eavesdropping" on them electronically. Are you open to having them give you a tour of their social media accounts once a month, for instance? Would that make you feel secure enough? Do you have enough trust in your kid to loosen the reins a little?

Even if you are employing a lighter touch, you still want to be clear about the consequences for bad behavior. What will you do if you see something you don't like? Will you curtail your child's use, impose stricter rules, or help her figure out a way to repair the damage done by her misstep? What if your child has expressed regret to you about the misstep? Can you turn it into a learning experience by making him do the work of fixing his mistake?

I'll stress once more that, whether you choose to spy, not spy, or use a blended approach, covertly accessing their accounts is not the way to go unless you are in a *code red* emergency (someone's life or safety is at stake). You'll encounter some difficulties no matter which approach you take. It's part of parenting. But starting from a place of honesty and openness sets the tone for your relationship with your child. Even if you consider technology one of life's add-ons, the way you use it is an expression of your values and, ultimately, an opportunity to build trust.

The Pressures of Being Always On

We all feel the pressures of a society that seems to never stop. It can be invigorating, on one hand, but exhausting on the other. Unlike you and me, our kids were born into this pace. They don't know another way. What's it like for them?

When I speak with middle schoolers, I always say, "Tell me what it's like to be an eleven-year-old with a smartphone and access to that much information." Or I say, "Tell me what it's like to be the last kid in your class to get a smartphone. Or the first one." These ten- to twelve-year-olds have thoughtful, high-level insights. Their answers might surprise you.

I worked with kids to cocreate solutions for some of the problems they see in their day-to-day lives. The conversations we had showed me that these kids are creative and insightful, and they exhibit a lot of empathy for others. That's great to hear, but it was also obvious that they need good models and help navigating their world. Just because they are digital natives doesn't mean that they are born digitally literate.

Start from a Place of Empathy

The most prevalent problem kids report is that they feel like they need to be accessible at all times. Because technology allows for it, they feel an obligation. It's easy for most of us to relate—you probably feel the same pressure in your own life!

The fact that we're human and can't always respond instantly is really challenging to navigate. For a teen or tween who's still learning the ins and outs of social interactions, it's even worse. Here's how this behavior plays out sometimes: your child texts one of his friends, and the friend doesn't text back right away. Now it's easy for your child to think, "This person doesn't want to be my friend anymore!" So he texts again, and again, and again. You can see how this could happen. Some of us may know adults who have this problem.

Again, we need to get curious about the child's experience. What could his friend be doing at this moment? The least likely possibility is that he doesn't want to be friends anymore. The most likely possibility is that the friend is busy doing something else. He's sleeping, he's doing his homework, he's eating dinner with his parents. Just by having this conversation about other possibilities with our child, we're raising his level of empathy.

If we want to go a step further, we can cocreate a solution. I did this with a creative group of fifth graders, suggesting that they design an app to help solve some of their social challenges. It wasn't a real app—it was just a prototype. But the exercise helped them understand the issues at play, and what they could do about them.

For this particular situation (nonresponse to a text), the kids came up with a great solution by positing an app that limits the number of texts you can send when they're not responded to within a certain window of time. They called it the "Text Lock" app. So if I start texting somebody, I can only text her so many times, and if she doesn't respond, I have to stop—the app forces me to. You can't buy this in the app store to deal with your annoying friend, but the solution is very revealing about kids' problems. They feel pressure from the constant accessibility of peers, and they feel that they are expected to be available and responsive at all times. We need to understand that kids feel this way, so we can help them set boundaries with their friends in a way that alleviates some of that pressure.

We can also help kids develop empathy so they put less pressure on their friends to be constantly responsive. In my workshops, I tell the kids, "Just close your eyes and imagine your friend doing her homework, or shooting some hoops in the driveway with her dad, or eating dinner with her family, and you'll be okay. You'll realize that she just can't get back to you right now." And that's really helpful for the kids. They don't need "Text Lock." Empathy is the app.

Sparkle Chat: The Solution for Not-Nice Texts

Kids in my workshops identified another problem they encounter frequently: what to do when they receive a text that is not so nice. Or what about when a person sends a text and it hurts a friend's or family member's feelings unintentionally? The kids in my workshops have all received messages they found upsetting—or have sent messages that offended others. It is good to remind our children that tone isn't always apparent when we text or post to social media. Because we can't see the other person, it can be hard to tell if he is being funny or serious, mean or joking—some important context is missing.

So we designed an app! A group of sixth graders at a girls' school invented an app they called "Sparkle Chat" that asks a very important question when a communication is typed into a device: "Are you sure you want to send that?" We could all use a reminder like that sometimes! What a great idea, and, again, so revealing. The kids even went so far as to design different levels; the more intense version of the app checked the message even after you clicked through the "Are you sure you want to send that?" warning. If the app detected some mean language, it would automatically send a copy to both the recipient's parents and the sender's parents.

Even though I am a parent, I could not have designed a more parental app for kids learning how to communicate with one another! This suggests that, even though the kids have tech savvy, they still need our mentorship. They need us to understand how easy it is to hurt someone's feelings (or to be hurt yourself) more than they need us to use monitoring software or to read all their texts. They need us to help them figure out what to do when things go wrong in a communication—and how can they can avoid it, if possible. And they do want to have the option to access adult support if a peer hurts their feelings.

Plugged-In Parents

Kids often complain that their parents are constantly plugged in too. When I ask about the problems in their lives that technology exacerbates, every single sixth and seventh grader answers the same way: they all say that the most important people in their lives are often inaccessible because of technology. As a parent, it kills me to hear this.

When we're glued to our smartphones or engrossed in e-mail, our kids feel like they're not needed. Again, they designed an app to fix the problem. Students in my workshops came up with an app called "Stop Texting, Enjoy Life" for their parents. Here's how it works. This app is voice-activated, and, when triggered by the child's voice, it actually shuts down mom or dad's phone.

The kids were clever enough to design the app so that it could be "trained" to recognize only the child's voice, so that random kids couldn't go up to adults on the street and turn off their phones. Clever, but perhaps a bit aggressive. That's where empathy comes in. As parents, we have put timers on our kids' use of technology, and these clever kids are letting us know that they want the same consideration. They want to feel important to you, not pushed aside by the demands of today's world and deprioritized by your accessibility to everyone else.

Even more depressing than the little kids who feel they have to demand their parents' attention are the teenagers who have given up. In *Reclaiming Conversation*, Sherry Turkle cites numerous teenagers and young adults who feel that they can't compete with their parents' smartphones, so they stop trying. Turkle describes the tog-gling back and forth between texting and conversation or e-mail and face-to-face time in families, and explores the cost to relation-ships: One young person reported, "When I am talking to my mom and she's e-mailing someone, she's like, 'wait' or she's talking to me and she stops her sentence in the middle to finish her meal and then keeps talking. And then stops and starts."[5] A young man Turkle interviewed explained that his parents have house rules against phones at the table but break them frequently, and then offer only short answers to his questions as their attention is often divided. A fifteen-year-old in Turkle's study says, "I think my mom has forgot-ten how to talk."[6] Ouch. None of us would want our children to say that about us, but we all need to remember that the people in the room are more important than the people buzzing in our pocket or in our hand.

If you need a wake-up call, let this be your moment. We all need to find a way to reduce the toggling we do between face-to-face communication and our devices, so we can truly engage and com-municate with our spouses, children, friends, and colleagues. While a "Stop Texting, Enjoy Life" app doesn't exist, you can picture the app in your head. When your children are trying to speak to you, look them in the eyes and listen. If you need to, tell yourself: "Okay, S.T.E.L., Stop Texting, Enjoy Life. I'm here. I'm present now."

Technology As a Window

What I love about the app-design exercise is that it tells us a lot about kids' day-to-day experience with technology. They do want our attention. They may seem like they don't—especially when they're at the age when they are getting their own mobile devices—but they want our attention, and they need our mentorship.

One of the eleven-year-olds who designed the "Text Lock" app asked in the session, "Is it okay if sometimes I just don't feel like texting?" I found this to be heartbreaking. Of course it's okay. We don't have to be plugged in all the time.

Despite all the kids' clever app ideas, there is no app that can raise kids in the digital age for us. The made-up ones above can't do it, nor can the real ones that exist in the app store today. Instead, we need to stay curious about kids' day-to-day experiences. Dive in and experience their digital world with them. Ask them what they're thinking and then sit down with them to cocreate solutions that take advantage of their creativity and your wisdom.

CHAPTER 6

Family Life in the Digital Age

When we become curious about our kids' day-to-day lives, we can better understand the challenges they face navigating the digital connectedness of their school and social world. Nonetheless, 24–7 connectivity with the outside world can put a strain on family life. Parents may find that they have few opportunities to model good communication for children and mentor them to be good communicators using cell phones, computers, and other digital media because these devices tend to be used privately; family members are not communicating out loud in one another's presence, as they did with a centrally located home telephone.

As great as technology can be for connection, it also presents some serious parenting challenges. These devices make it easier for us to be in frequent contact with our kids, but they also give kids access to a whole world we don't know about. As journalist Jennifer Senior says, "They are hyperconnected to their families. But they also lead lives quite separate and apart."[1] Whether we approach technology with strict limits and prohibitions or with a mentorship mindset, navigating that constant contact amid the reality of kids' separate lives with their peers can be difficult.

Further, according to researcher Sherry Turkle, who has spent

her career examining how technology affects interpersonal relationships, many families are now navigating via text messages conflicts
that might once have involved yelling or hushed, late-night conversations.[2] While the families in Turkle's study found it "cleaner" to
consider conflict at a remove, she wonders if the spontaneity and the
messiness of real, in-your-face feelings that emerge quickly might be
something we should be afraid to lose. It's an interesting question to
ponder about our own families—should we keep it quiet or keep it
real?

Just as we don't want our kids to become unable to socialize face
to face, we don't want to become unable to negotiate conflicts with
our kids face to face. On the other hand, a kind text might have
its place in a tense situation when the person we're arguing with
can't summon himself to hear us. When I asked parents in my Raising Digital Natives community if they ever take conflicts to text
or e-mail, the answers were across the board. One mother said, "I
don't. No way. I might text 'I love you' to the kids to tide me over
until we are face to face and I can give 'em a big squeeze and then
discuss." Another mom said, "I do both. Sometimes I'll send a quick
text, but always follow up with a convo." One teenager said he had
made up with his mother after yelling at her on the ride to school
with a texted "I am sorry I was an ass@#$," and that she appreci-
ated it, although he also acknowledged that an in-person apology is
generally best and most sincere.

Because opportunities to model good communication habits
may be scarce now that family telephones aren't centrally located
in the house, you may wish to consciously talk through some of
your choices. Say, "I am going to leave my phone turned off and in
the other room during dinner and family time so that I don't get
distracted." Or, "I am going to send this e-mail but I don't want to
bother someone at this hour, so I'll schedule it to send tomorrow

morning." Letting your kids see the reasoning behind each of your choices is a great way for them to learn.

Watch Yourself... Your Kids Are

Kids learn their values and behaviors from watching us. Are you texting when your kids are talking to you? Are you checking your e-mails while they are around? Are you "allowed" to answer your phone during dinner and blame it on work?

The pressures of today's constantly connected world seem to put us in a perpetual state of multitasking. I feel the same pressure, so I have a lot of sympathy for the challenges. But what does this say to our kids? Can we set a better example?

If you can commit to not checking your phone constantly, you will send a powerful message to your kids. You are in control, not controlled by your devices. The boundaries you set and adhere to will not only free you, they will also set an example for your kids. In other words, if you put your cell phone away during important family time, they will too. When you show your kids that family time is important, they will come to value it also. Many of us check e-mail hundreds of times a day. Productivity experts and family experts agree—this doesn't help your productivity or your relationships. If you text at dinner, don't expect your tween or teen to leave his phone somewhere else or turn it off.

Modeling a balanced use of your own devices may be the most important message you can send your child about the role of technology in your family. Try going to the park or playground tech-free. Curb your own tech use at mealtimes—and during other family time. Find a family "safe word" that is funny but serves as a good reminder. In my house, we are allowed to nicely call one another out for being "screen monsters," and we remind each other to "be here now."

We've all seen families and friends eating lunch while checking their smartphones. It's a scene we've witnessed in restaurants, and it always looks worse on others, doesn't it? Either on your own, or with your spouse/partner, take a mental inventory of your own family's "Alone Together" time.[3] Notice whether your family is spending a lot of time in the same physical space but each looking at his or her own screen. You have to be mindful and objective, as often time together is not planned this way. But as you look back on the past week, or at any typical week, do you find members of the family in their own corners, or even right next to one another, absorbed in their individual digital worlds?

Journalist Susan Maushart unplugged her entire family—herself and her three teenage children—for six months. While the kids were initially resentful, Maushart found that the siblings grew closer to one another (and not purely because they were upset with their mother!) and that old talents and hobbies, notably her son's talent at a musical instrument, resurfaced when video games and texting did not eat up so much free time. While full unplugging is a radical step, becoming more mindful of the way family time can be eroded by the pull of networked connections can help your family stay connected. Maushart's book about her family's experience, *The Winter of Our Disconnect,* might just offer you the inspiration you need to look up from your routine and notice your own family's habits.[4]

The next exercise may not be fun for you, but ask your children which of your tech habits is their least favorite. You may already know your own weaknesses, but it can be really helpful to get your kids' view. What do you do when a family member wants to talk with you? Do you close your laptop or put down your phone? If you watched a video of yourself, would it surprise you? Would you like what you see? I struggle with this as a full-time consultant and speaker, because the boundaries around work are a little different than they might be with a nine-to-five job. Even so, many parents with jobs that are technically nine to five are expected to be constantly accessible—and they find it to be just as much of a challenge. What can you do to change habits around media use? Look for opportunities for unplugged time or for shared media use, such as watching a movie together. The introverts in your family may depend on "alone" tech time to replenish from social time. If that describes you (or another family member), think about whether there are other activities that may foster some true solitude to replenish that introverted side.

Building a Media Ecology

I often present to parent groups on the topic of "building a media ecology in your home." The audience is generally made up of parents of three- to nine-year-olds, and the presentation always precipitates a number of wonderful conversations afterward—but one in particular really made me think. First of all, this conversation happened with a dad. At many parent talks I've offered, the audience has been about 80 percent moms, so I am always delighted to see a more even split. This particular dad started out by thanking me for not making him feel like a bad parent in my talk. This is so important to me—I believe that judging other parents prevents us from building strong communities where we all watch out for one another's kids.

This father's question was about eating in front of the TV. He wondered whether it would harm his children's minds or their social skills if they ate some of their meals while watching a TV show. In their household, children are allowed to eat while watching TV as a treat, or at times when the parents want a little adult time over dinner. This is a hard question to answer definitively, as my goal is to help families do what works for them. But I do believe that family meals are important for teaching kids social skills. Not only is dinnertime conversation a good way to check in with your children's world, but it also models adult behavior and lets kids see us engage fully in our own relationships.

Yet the desire to sit down with your partner or spouse for a quiet meal is understandable, and you don't want to have to wait until your kids leave for college! I have two suggestions for handling this:

1. **Unplugged meals.** Focus on having "unplugged" family meals at certain times. It doesn't have to be every meal. Perhaps a few meals could involve the kids watching TV while parents eat and catch up. This might give the family energy for some unplugged meals at which they all sit down together and talk.

2. **The two-shift approach.** An alternative is to feed the kids a sit-down meal that is not in front of a screen before the adults eat. You can talk with them, and have them sit for whatever time is developmentally reasonable, and then you can "release them" to a TV show or game while you eat. Early dinner for children was a tradition in some families and can still work when parents get home from work too late for the children's schedule.

Fans of "mindful eating" would probably prefer the two-shift approach to dinner, because it involves postponing media time until after a meal. Eating while you are distracted can be associated with unhealthy eating choices. I think the most important thing to do is to create some unplugged meal rituals that you stick to so that kids can get used to them and actually start to look forward to them!

The ideal of a family dinner is difficult to reconcile with the reality of exhausting weekdays followed by evenings filled with homework for both kids and adults. While a peaceful, media-free family dinner may seem like an unattainable goal, taking the first step toward being intentional about mealtimes will help. Pick one of these approaches and try it out one night this week.

Always check yourself. Are you modeling focused conversation and good eye contact, and are you turning off devices during family time? If not, it will be very difficult to get your teen or tween to unplug—ever.

The New Family Album

The proliferation of images made possible by digital photography has had a huge cultural impact. Digital images are now a form of communication, yet we as a culture haven't fully written new rules. The ease with which these images are created and shared can be joyful and enriching, but photos shared freely can also cause friction and hurt feelings. In that way, photo sharing is no different from any other form of communication.

As I mentioned in chapter 4, every member of the family should follow the same rule about posting or sharing images of other family members: don't do it without permission. Asking your kids before sharing pictures of them teaches your children that you respect them and their privacy. This practice also brings up an opportunity to discuss boundaries. Kids are allowed to tell you that they don't want you to post a particular picture of them, and the reason doesn't matter. Allow them to assert some control over this—it's a hugely valuable lesson for them to learn.

Let's look at how photos might be handled at a social event. Kids' birthday parties are a great opportunity for us to model and teach kids about what's okay to share widely—and what is not. Depending on their age and maturity level, some kids with whom I work understand that there's a difference between taking a picture and sharing a picture. They get that kids who were not invited might feel hurt if they see pictures of the party posted on Instagram, for instance.

Now, this doesn't mean you can't take pictures; it just means you should think about how sharing them on social media might make others feel. As always, modeling empathy in thoughtful sharing can help your child save other kids from hurt feelings.

What About Other Family Members?

Grandparents, aunts and uncles, and close family friends all mean well. They love your kids, and they cherish watching them grow up. But their level of interest may not be matched by others. For instance, your child's grandparents might have an unlimited appetite for photos of your kids, but your high school friends on Facebook or your work buddies may have a more modest interest. To mitigate this mismatch, parents can find alternatives to social media for their family albums:

- Use Dropbox, Box, or Google Drive.
- Load photos onto a password-protected website, such as Flickr, that offers control over how public your photographs are, and whether you want to offer them for others to use via a Creative Commons license.
- E-mail to share more regularly with the inner circle of people who really do want those weekly pics!

The rest of the people with whom you socialize online will be grateful, if they haven't hidden you already! An added benefit is that your kids' smaller digital footprint may be something they appreciate one day. Three hundred people don't need weekly pictures of your children, I promise. You can create a family social media policy to help reinforce the different levels of sharing.[5] I love the one technology researcher Alexandra Samuel created for her family (alexandrasamuel.com/parenting/creating-a-family-social-media-policy). If you do implement a family social media policy, remember to include yourself in the plan. Some parents choose not to share about their children on Facebook, Twitter, and other social spaces. But if you do post about your children, how can you respect their privacy and boundaries as well as teach them about empathy for both the viewers and the subject of the photographs? If your child is old enough to understand the idea of photos being shared, you should ask her permission before sharing pictures. If your child is too young for you to ask, imagine her as a privacy-oriented twelve-, fifteen-, or thirty-year-old. Might she have an objection? If so, reconsider.

Start teaching empathy and respect regarding photo sharing as early as you can. Giving your child a new device can be a great occasion to open this discussion—start with training wheels in the form of boundaries and expectations. This conversation will also prompt you to examine your own relationship to the digital tools and toys already in your home.

Curating Your Family's Media Experiences

Putting in place the right structures, routines, and physical organization regarding media use will ultimately make it easier to support the family life you want. You likely already have such structures in place in other arenas. For instance, you might put away seasonally inappropriate clothes to foster a six-year-old's independence in choosing his own clothes, while still ensuring that he doesn't go to school in shorts when it is twenty degrees outside. You can set up habits, routines, and a physical organization in your home that makes it easier to balance the use of technology. I call this a "media ecology," and the way you create it can make a huge positive impact on your home.

Creating Attractive Unplugged Zones

One of these most effective ways to reduce dependence on electronics is to make offline time more enticing. With a little planning and creativity, you can design appealing unplugged zones in your home to lure your kids away from their iPads and PlayStations. The screens will always be attractive, so even if you put them in the least comfy location, kids and adults will gravitate to them.

Make sure that the comfiest, coziest spots in your house are not just the ones with adjacent screens. Set up spaces that encourage your kids to be creators, not just consumers. Make stuff together with your child, online and offline. In the digital realm, you can make a family scrapbook, design a video game, develop a scavenger hunt, make a calendar for Grandma, write some code in Scratch, or make a video to post on YouTube.

Offline, you can build a model of your dream city, make some cookies, or sew a patch on your favorite jeans. You don't need a big space for this. One corner of our dining room is set up as an art area, complete with a bin of art supplies and a desk. Another great activity is finding broken things in your house and learning to fix them by watching YouTube videos.

Beyond your home environment, there are plenty of opportunities to get creative. If your child is a crafty-makey, take-apart kind of kid, or you want to encourage this, take her to a Maker Faire, a festival at which people show and share the things they've made. Send her to camp to learn to build robots, design costumes, or write computer code. Or make it possible for her to do those things at home. In my own community, pop-up playgrounds, where families bring cardboard and other fun building materials, are catching on as a way to encourage kids to interact with materials and other people in new ways.

For young kids, make sure the TV, video games, and computers are not taking over the most comfortable and attractive zones in your home. Stock an accessible kitchen drawer with fun supplies, and change them regularly so your children will be surprised. Make the dress-up clothes, cool games, new puzzles, and art supplies as accessible as the TV, gaming devices, and tablets.

Help bigger kids tap into their own creativity. Fill a box with recycled stuff so they can make things. Think about keeping musical instruments, recipe books, and cooking supplies on hand. Let them get messy in the kitchen with their friends making pizza or cupcakes. Challenge them to create a scavenger hunt or an obstacle course—with the family or their friends.

If mobile devices are loose in your home, you may want kids (and even adults?) to use them in public spaces rather than burrowing into their bedrooms or the basement. A communal charging station underscores the message that devices are not for snuggling with at night. As an added benefit, you are less likely to find yourself running out the door with an uncharged device in the morning!

Structure Is Your Friend

Structuring physical space and schedules thoughtfully can help ease tensions. Use habits and routines to minimize post-screen-time tantrums and flipouts. Don't let screen time be an unstructured period that fits in around everything else. If your kids love Minecraft, they can have their specific Minecraft time. Try making a calendar. Plan what they will do *after* their immersive screen experience. If they turn into "screen monsters" and act unpleasant when their time is over, let them know you'll be dialing back their time in fifteen minute increments until they can refrain from turning into monsters. Many families have decided on minimal to zero screen time during the week because the transitions are too much to manage, along with the demands of school, homework, and after-school activities. That's fine, too, of course. You have to find the right balance for your family and your kid's temperament. And remember, changes to any routine take time. Have patience, stick with your plan, and adjust as necessary until you find the right balance.

Media As a Conversation Starter for Big Issues

We as parents can cultivate social consciousness in our kids through media literacy. Engage with them about stereotypes in media without raining on their parade. Instead of insisting, "That show is sexist," ask your kids what they think about the male and female characters, or about the way characters of different ethnicities are portrayed.

Try to also stock your media library with girl heroes, smart characters of color, etc. It won't be easy, but the offerings have gotten better in recent years. Sites like A Mighty Girl (amightygirl.com) can be a great resource—and not just for parents raising girls!

If you simply hate a show, character, genre, or company—and especially if you prohibit it—tell your children why. "Because I said so" may have been the way of our parents' generation, but explaining your reasoning is likely to yield better results; kids are more able to follow rules they understand.[6]

Even if your kids sneak around your ban, they will know that the way people act toward one another on a certain program bothers you. For instance, you don't like the way characters use one another for financial or sexual gain, but it doesn't bother you that the main character's brother is gay.

Be really specific, so they know and understand your reasoning. Many contemporary shows—even the ones for kids—put challenging issues on the table. Issues such as teenage sexuality, drugs, abusive relationships, and eating disorders are thorny problems for all ages.

While the week-to-week churn of trauma may seem a bit much, some of these issue-oriented shows can provide opportunities to talk about these matters with your children. Even when it's uncomfortable, more communication is a positive thing. Tweens in particular are taking in all the info they can as they form their identities, and you want to be there to help guide them and influence their values. Choose your moments strategically, though. If you start a deep conversation every time with every show, your children may not enjoy watching TV with you. But calling their attention to media portrayals as part of a deeper discussion of issues like racism and sexism will make them more informed, more critical viewers.

Family Communication

One of the most common questions parents ask me is when they should allow their children to have their own cell phone or smartphone. Many parents wish they could connect with their children when they are running a few minutes late to pick them up, when it is time to collect them from a game or a friend's house, or in similar scenarios. And Mike Lanza, author of *Playborhood,* points out that in some ways, cell phones give kids independence.[7] But, while we may get kids their first device so we can communicate with them, unless we give them a very locked-down device, we are also opening up new worlds of peer communication (and, in the case of a smartphone, the whole Internet).

A recent thread on one of the parenting Facebook groups I participate in started with the query, "What is the going age for getting your child a cell phone these days?" The varied responses poured in quickly. Many parents thought a child's ability to travel independently in the community—either biking or taking public transit to school—was a useful marker. Other parents said they felt they "had" to get kids a phone when their friends got them. Answers varied from wrist devices that only called Mom and Dad or basic flip phones for fourth graders to "no phone until eighth grade" policies, as well as responses from a host of parents who had gotten smartphones for sixth or seventh graders.

As the responses to this thread reveal, getting a phone for your child is a decision that you want to make with her maturity in mind. Smartphones have an especially high impact, although "dumb" cell phones are a big responsibility too, even though they don't come with same number of distractions and responsibilities that a smartphone does. Many parents on the thread felt that a cell phone would suffice for their middle schooler and preferred to wait until eighth grade or high school before they purchased a smartphone for their child. But in the many affluent private and public schools where I work, the first phone is often a smartphone, and it might be given in fifth or sixth grade.

When Is Your Child Ready for a Phone?

Getting a phone for your child is one of the biggest decisions you will make as a parent. If you think that's an overstatement, think about this: the first smartphone is a turning point, a door that opens the entire world to your child. She will now have complete access to the Internet and the ability be in contact with almost anyone on the planet—from anywhere. All this can potentially happen away from your watchful eye. While that may sound scary, there are a lot of positives about this newfound power. But it's exactly why I am so bullish on the importance of mentorship. Teaching your child to make good decisions is better protection than anything else you can do for your child.

Start with Your Own Fears

The issues surrounding cell phones, and the appropriate time for a child to have one of her own, can be fraught, which is why it's important to examine your concerns. What exactly are your fears about getting your child a cell phone or smartphone? Conversely, what are your fears about not getting one for your child? Are you worried that she will be the only one in her social group without a phone? That she might be ostracized? That you will be *that* mom who wouldn't let her kid get a cell phone? Or are you simply worried that without it she won't be able to communicate with you throughout the day?

Here is a roster of the key issues for you to think about:

1. **Social issues.** Without a cell phone, your child could be out of the loop—cut off from social circles. But if your child does have a phone, you might worry that she will become screen addicted and withdraw from family contact. Or that she will lose lose face-to-face social skills because she relies on devices for communication. Or that she will be tempted to overshare to gain social standing.

2. **Status issues.** An iPhone, for example, can be viewed as a status symbol. You don't want it to appear that your family can't afford a phone. On the other hand, you may not want your child to

be the only one in school who has an iPhone. Contextual cues are important because the digital landscape is different, depending on the area where you live.

3. **Safety issues.** Pornography and other inappropriate content will be more accessible on a smartphone. Parents wonder, can my child resist the pull? Beyond that, parents worry that there's more potential for contact with strangers through smartphone apps, chat, and online. Will your child make sound, healthy decisions?

4. **Privacy issues.** Every phone now comes with a camera built in. This increases the chances that inappropriate photos will be taken or shared. And what about the information/data trail that your child is leaving? All posts and interactions build up a digital footprint. Does your child understand the larger issues of digital identity?

When you put all these together, it's easy to see why cell phone use—and especially smartphone use—is such a source of stress for families. Let's look at some examples, and then at some criteria for making your own decision about when (and how) to manage this turning point.

Stories from the Battlefield

One mother, "Dominique," from a group I was working with, has a highly responsible daughter, and Dominique enjoys a trusting relationship with her. One night, Dominique found out that her daughter, "Anne," was texting a friend late at night when she (and her friend) should have been sleeping. The friend felt that she needed help, and Anne felt she couldn't say no. Dominique decided that from then on, the cell phone would be kept in the parents' room overnight. She also decided to let the other girl's parents know, since the girls were both only twelve years old (in sixth grade). First, it is important that Dominique learn the reason Anne felt she had to respond to her friend at a late hour. This way, Dominique could be aware of her daughter's attempts to be a supportive friend, and could also discuss with her the kinds of issues that might require some adult assistance, not just the counsel of a fellow sixth grader. Understanding the positive impulses that might cause a child to break our rules helps us respond appropriately.

One mother in my Raising Digital Natives community purchased phones for both her ten-year-old and her eleven-year-old when they started riding the bus to school rather than being driven; she said, "For my ten-year-old [there was] almost no change in her life. She forgets it one day out of two. The eleven-year-old took more to it. She 'lost' the privilege for one week after I discovered her texting at 10 p.m. one of the rare nights where the phone was not charging in our kitchen, and she came with some interesting conclusions on her own on how the phone was impacting the relationship with her sister. After one day without her phone she came home to say that not having a phone enabled her to socialize more with her sister on the school bus."

Another mother said she wanted her kids to take financial responsibility for their phones: "I want my kids to be able to pay for the monthly phone bill before considering buying them a phone. My thirteen-year-old has an iPod and has figured out how to get an app for calling and texting that works with Wi-Fi. We have a home phone for when they are home after school or home alone. My eleven-year-old daughter has a phone from her dad (not my choice), but she is so paranoid about going over plan, it seems to be okay for her. My kids have a lot of independence, i.e., being home after school for a couple hours. We do weekly family meetings to keep communication and expectations clear."

Another child in the pediatric practice of one of my acquaintances was grounded from cell phone use and became excessively panicked. She was sobbing uncontrollably and visibly scared. After close questioning, the girl confessed that another student was blackmailing her for revealing photos, and said that if she didn't send more he'd share the original ones widely. Yikes! Once the parents were aware of the situation, they got some counseling for their daughter and blocked the solicitor of the revealing pictures. They could have taken criminal action, but in this case, chose not to. Another approach, if the aggressor is known and is a minor, is contacting the child's parents. Families that pursue legal remedies for challenges like this are potentially taking an important step toward stopping online predators from repeating this behavior. On the other hand, prosecuting these cases can be immensely difficult, and the law is far behind in terms of possible abuses and incursions in the digital arena.

One of the most important things for your child to know is that no one should pressure her (or him) to do something she feels is wrong or is uncomfortable doing. Not a stranger, friend, boyfriend, girlfriend, and so on. She also needs to know that, even if she has broken some of your rules (e.g., texting after hours, making a bad decision), you are her ally and support if she is being harassed or is in trouble. This is critical!

The examples I've just laid out teach us an important lesson— look to the ways other parents handle difficult situations. We all learn from one another. How would you have handled the situations above? Maybe not the same way the parents described did. That's okay. We each have our own parenting style. But it helps to see what others are doing so you have a frame of reference.

Before You Buy Technology

Many parents buy their children cell phones so they can check in, but before you do this, ask yourself if this is your desire or theirs. Do you need to check in? What are some of the situations you've experienced where you wished you had this capability? Many of us now run late with less stress knowing we can text that we are on our way. When our kids don't have phones, running late may feel like it's less of an option.

So, are you ready or not? Should you or shouldn't you get your child a cell phone? If not now, when is the right time for your family? I wish I had an easy all-encompassing answer to these questions, but this issue is nuanced and individualized. However, I created this road map to help you decide if and when it's time:

1. **Get clear on what your real fears and desires are.** One family I know wanted their kids to have more independence and to roam "free range." Though their urban neighborhood was friendly and close-knit, they still felt that safety demanded a little more communication than simply, "Come home when the street lights come on." Their solution? They gave their kids (ages six and nine) walkie-talkies. A few other neighborhood parents followed suit. Now, the neighborhood kids were free to play, but they were virtually connected to home by the range of their walkie-talkies. A good solution!

2. **Check in about the reasons your child wants the phone.** Is the phone predominantly a prop for fitting in, or are other kids actually making plans on their phones and leaving your child out? If this is happening, talk to other kids' parents—especially those in

your child's inner circle—so they know they can text you to include your son or daughter.

3. **Teach kids some basic phone etiquette.** Before kids get their own phone, make sure they know how to answer a phone, make a call, and leave a message politely. You would do this with a "regular" phone, too—a cell phone is no different. Have your child practice with a grandparent, aunt or uncle, or close family friend. Ask this person to call your cell phone, but have your child answer. Practice until she answers smoothly and appropriately. Do the same for outgoing calls, having her practice initiating calls until she gets the hang of the interaction. The "advanced level" is to have your child order a pizza or call a store to get business hours.

E-Mail Training Wheels

E-mail is now such a part of our lives that it seems second nature to us. For many of us, it's the primary way we communicate in the workplace. Because e-mail use seems so basic, it may feel like you don't need to teach your kids anything about it.

But e-mail is still a form of communication, and it has its own unwritten rules and code of etiquette. And, as you've probably experienced in the workplace, e-mail can go wrong very easily. It's worth taking the time to give your child the fundamentals so that she knows how to navigate the medium properly. It's an important bridge between your child, her teachers, and the adult world, and—let's face it—she probably won't be Snapchatting her future employer. She'll be e-mailing, at least for now. So this is something that you want to get right.

My advice when introducing any new technology to your kids is to give them "training wheels." Before you allow your kid to have his own e-mail, let him try using a family e-mail account. For example, set up an account such as TengFamily@gmail.com or TheThompsons@yahoo.com. This centralized account works a bit like a landline in the kitchen. You are not spying, but the account is "public," at least in the household. After all, it is a shared account. As with a shared telephone, you'll get the chance to make sure your child learns proper salutations and closings. And it will give you the chance to watch how he interacts and jump in with helpful advice when you see a misstep. Obviously, you'll want to do this with a light touch. Push too hard, and your advice will feel like criticism.

Lastly, don't forget to make sure that your kids, your extended family, and even your children's friends know that e-mail sent to this address goes to everyone in your family. Context is incredibly important in communication, and it's unfair to surprise people with a wider readership than they were expecting. Your goal is not to catch your kid or her friends in a gotcha moment, it's to teach good digital citizenship.

Moneywise

Kids in the Internet age seem to range from clueless novices to savvy web entrepreneurs. Your kids are probably somewhere in the middle. The minute they ask to make an Internet purchase, download an app, or upgrade from a freemium model, you need to start talking about digital money. Indeed, it is very easy to get sucked into online purchasing, and the relatively low prices of apps and in-app purchases can create unpleasant surprises when the bills come in. In-app purchases are a scourge for parents of both younger and older kids. You always want to disable these (at least to start), and the games that constantly demand such buys may not be the games you want available, or on heavy rotation, among your children. While marketing laws determine that certain products can't be advertised during kids' shows, in-app purchase prompts seem to get around this restriction. They are attractive because they are strategically placed—right when you are about to get to the next level. When the rush of endorphins kicks in, you're much more tempted to spend real money on not-real gold "coins." These offers are very hard to resist and can add up in insidious ways. If a young child has generated a huge bill without your knowledge or consent, you may be able to get a refund from the company. Then, change your settings and talk to your child.

Money in the digital world and as represented by debit and credit cards can be quite abstract. I find myself less sensitive to small purchases of apps than I am to physical things, as I dread clutter. In the physical world, I always think about where we will put that new toy or game. But "the cloud" has endless shelf space. On the other hand, you can apply a similar question to a new application—what role does it play in my life? If you already have a drawing app, how is this one different? Clutter is still clutter, even in the digital world.

I asked a number of parents in my Raising Digital Natives community for their recommendations on how to mentor kids about money in the digital age. One mother shared that her seventh grader spends as much as $30 per day on coffee and snacks with her friends when they go to Starbucks or the mall after school. The mom knows what her daughter is spending because the daughter has a debit card. Reviewing the statements together (and making the daughter responsible for paying her own bills) might help her spend more frugally. If not, putting a limit on the card—or letting the daughter actually run out of cash in her account—could be a wake-up call. The mother, a successful business owner, would think twice before spending $30 on lunch. The fact that her thirteen-year-old is such a casual spender suggests she hasn't connected the dots yet, and that the money does not translate in her mind to labor or struggle of any kind.

Another mother offered some strategies for teaching financial literacy:

> I started giving my eight-year-old an allowance this year, and do it through the website Famzoo, which I love. It's been a great experience teaching him about managing money and spending. I have allowed him to spend money on "apps" if they are appropriate—and if he has the funds, of course. He has frequently asked me if he can buy "in-app purchases," and I've drawn the line on that as I just don't want him spending allowance money to buy points in some silly online game. It's a tough distinction to explain to an eight-year-old. It's okay to buy a (dumb) game like Angry Birds, but I don't want him spending money to "advance a level" in the game.

It's easy to see why a parent wouldn't want her kids to spend money on things that lack a physical presence. It seems frivolous, even if it's important to our kids. Another mother decided to try a cash allowance for now: "We used to use a virtual allowance called 'Moneytrail' and take money out for online purchases like apps and iTunes, but it didn't work out. Kids never saw the money, and so it was less tangible for them. We've just recently (two weeks ago) switched back to cash for the allowance."

For older kids who have bank accounts, do they know how to access that information online? Teaching kids about secure passwords is critical. While we might take that necessity for granted, kids might not yet have a full understanding of the ramifications of an insecure account.

You may wish to give your kids a digital allowance for buying apps, books, and music, too. Another mother says: "My eldest (eleven) is the only one with his own tablet. He has an iTunes user account linked to ours (in the family cloud) and when he sees an app, song, or e-book he'd like, he can ask for download and we will get a message about the request, which we then can approve or not. With apps in particular, we usually ask him what he wants it for or whether he has checked if it's free or not. And we then check with him whether he has to give personal info when registering. No other virtual buying among the 'iKids' for now."

Advanced Money Wisdom

Some families and schools encourage more advanced financial literacy. For instance, they follow the stock market online using resources like Morningstar or E-Trade. My nephew attends a public high school in New York City where some students' parents work on Wall Street. Students at his school can join an investment club challenge, and whoever ends the year with the most virtual money (no actual money is invested) wins a prize.

You can also teach your kids to research companies. Perhaps they wish to support companies that practice fair trade or take another ethical stance. On the other hand, I was slightly disturbed to hear about all the short-term trading that occurred in my nephew's investment club. Most real-life stockholders are investing past the end of the school year, so showing your kids some of your long-term growth on a mutual fund or CD might bring that lesson home more than a short-term investing contest.

If your kids are interested in selling things they make, opening a store on a site such as Etsy could be a great way to learn more about the new economy. If kids contribute without pay to sites such as

Wikipedia, talk with them about why we sometimes do work without getting paid, and how that can contribute to the greater good. Teaching children to bank online, and perhaps to set up accounts where they can pay for their own things with money they've saved (or been lucky enough to be given) is important. For many kids, middle school is an appropriate time to move from the physical reality of the piggy bank to basic online money management.

Children can learn to track their finances in apps such as Mint. And you can also give them a look at your own finances. Even if you prefer that they don't know your salary, sharing a pie chart of your family's expenses is a great way to help them understand why you have to work, what you spend your money on, and how you plan for expenses. Use this opportunity to show them how and why to save money, and help them appreciate the "extras" too! By middle school they can start to really grasp ideas like compound interest, savings, inflation, and so on.

Another parent in the Raising Digital Natives community talked about the proactive steps she and her husband are taking to introduce their daughter to financial responsibility: "We opened a checking account for our high schooler when she turned thirteen (credit to my mom for doing this with me in high school, too!). We deposit my daughter's clothing allowance, public transit card money, and payments for caring for her younger brother in the account. She deposits cash for other work and monetary gifts. She pays her expenses with her debit card. She is also responsible for balancing her checkbook (on Quicken) if she wants reimbursement for anything (like her transit card). She's become very conscious of the value of things, waits for sales to buy an item, etc."

Ron Lieber, *New York Times* personal finance columnist and the author of *The Opposite of Spoiled,* advises relative transparency around money questions and especially age-appropriate honesty in response to questions.[8] Children are interested in understanding not just how much you make but how much you spend. They might want to know your salary, their school tuition, or how much your house cost. In many cases, if they can search the Internet (i.e., if they are six or older) they may not need to ask you at all, as the information is readily available. As with topics like sex, it is better if they ask you about money. Be prepared for the day when your children come to you with personal financial information (like your salary or the price of your home) they learned from an Internet search and want to know more.

Financial Literacy (and Trust)

What is a realistic amount of trust to place in your kids when it comes to handling money? Do we ever want our kids to have access to our credit cards or to accounts with credit cards enabled? Would a child who would never take a bill out of your wallet use your password to order something? Have you been clear that permission is needed (in both cases)? Here are some questions to ask yourself:

- Do you know how to block your child from making online or in-app purchases?
- Is your iPad an unfettered path to Amazon? If you've given your kids your Amazon password to watch a movie or TV series, don't be surprised if they figure out they can make other purchases.
- Do you know how to manage a shared Apple ID? Many families in the Apple universe have found a shared Apple ID to be a mixed blessing. Anything downloaded ends up accessible to everyone, but a shared Apple ID tied to your credit card may feel like carte blanche to your children.

I recently had dinner with wonderful family friends who are raising three kind and thoughtful children. The middle child, a ninth grader, was discussing his fantasy football league, and in particular, how well he was doing. I asked (somewhat) innocently if they play for points or for money. As I know from adult friends and colleagues, money is often exchanged over fantasy football.

The young man said they were considering exchanging money, but they did not want to put cash in the mail. He played largely with friends from summer camp, and they were not local. So the teens were thinking about using PayPal. His father said, "No, you can't do that—no gambling for money." And the son said, jokingly, "So if we do it, I just won't tell you." Yikes.

This classic moment opened a conversation that probably continued when dinner guests were no longer in the house. There is a lot of well-earned trust between the grown-ups and children in this family, and I am sure they will continue the discussion. But it also points to an issue our parents simply did not have to deal with.

One approach the family could take is to say, "You cannot have access to a credit card to use PayPal, and I forbid you to link your bank account to PayPal." Another would be to let the kid experiment with gambling and potentially lose (or win) money. While for many kids the experience of losing or gaining a little money this way would be a learning experience, it could also be dangerous. And who sets limits on how much is okay to lose or win?

Ultimately, the parents should outline clearly what they will and won't allow, while acknowledging that their kid is capable of going behind their backs. They should be clear that they expect their son to keep their trust by doing the right thing.

This story brings up some of the challenges of leading a connected life. First, our children are used to Amazon boxes showing up with desired objects inside. It is very easy to lose track of spending, especially when our credit cards are enabled for one-touch ordering. To curb impulsivity, I purposely use difficult passwords that have to be looked up to access accounts like Amazon—this gives an additional moment of pause.

Connected Families

Family life in the digital age can be a lot of fun. It is fun to see faraway nieces and nephews on social media and to talk to grandparents via Skype. It can be fun to play Words with Friends with your mother-in-law and to text with your teenager. Setting up routines and curating the space at home can go a long way toward setting yourself up for success, so you don't have to police your kids' tech use—and they don't have to police yours! Use key milestones (a new year or birthdays) to check in to see if you are happy with the current balance of technology in your family and to reflect on what small (or large) changes you may want to make.

CHAPTER 7

Friendship and Dating in the Digital Age

Learning about friendship is one of the most crucial experiences our kids have as they grow up. The interactions and challenges that arise with friends as mediated by games, social media, group texts, or video chats are not wholly different from the challenges of navigating these relationships face to face, but there are some new social rules and nuances we can help our kids understand. Some young people also start having crushes and possibly dating in middle school or high school. As with friendships, these romantic relationships are not so different than young relationships have ever been (school dances are still terribly awkward, for instance), but they have new dimensions we need to consider. Here are some scenarios you may encounter:

- You've been holding out on getting your sixth grader a phone, but suddenly it seems like all her friends have one. They are all connected constantly, making plans, and your child doesn't want to be left out. You let her use your smartphone, but that plan has backfired—you are sick of getting text messages from twelve-year-olds. And no way will you give up your phone for your daughter's nightly group text party. Besides, you are still not convinced that this is the best way for her to connect with her friends.

• Many of your third grader's friends play an online game together after school. You want your son to do his homework and get some exercise after school, so you've limited his online gaming to weekends only. But he feels left out and says he is getting behind in the game. What's worse is that it seems to be affecting his offline friendships at school, too.

• Together, you and your eleven-year-old daughter are looking at her e-mail and you see auto responses from Twitter, Instagram, and several other social applications. You are angry because you thought you had an agreement that she would wait until she was thirteen to set up these accounts. On further examination, it becomes clear that the accounts belong to her best friend, a kid you've known for years. She just used your daughter's e-mail account to set them up, as her parents, who are generally stricter than you are, have not allowed her to have e-mail. How do you respond?

• Your son comes back from a Boy Scout trip having been shown texts—and possibly pictures—of a girl in the next grade that all the kids at school seem to talk about. He feels bad, because his friends on the bus were teasing him because he didn't want to look at the pictures.

Sometimes it feels like raising your kid with all this technology would be fine if it weren't for other kids! I'll describe some pitfalls to watch out for as your child's friendships grow and change, as well as some positive behaviors we want to model.

Healthy Friendships in the Digital World

Let's take a minute to outline what we're aiming for. Here is an ideal model of a kid who is ready to build and sustain healthy friendships in both the digital and face-to-face worlds:

- She understands the difference between an online and offline friend.
- She can be clear about her boundaries.
- She understands that popularity is not measured by how many Instagram followers you have.
- She is sensitive to issues of exclusion and can identify when it's happening.
- She understands how to use privacy settings to help manage her social profiles.
- She is safe and thoughtful in the way she handles dating and romantic relationships.
- She recognizes that conflicts will arise, but knows to take it offline when it happens.
- She can distinguish between run-of-the-mill hurt feelings and online cruelty.

Many of your children's experiences of friendship will resemble your own childhood experiences: finding a new best friend, spending lots of time together, and then maybe having a falling out. There's the ever-evolving group of friends and the internal jockeying for power within a clique. There's shyness and social missteps. And yes, there are still the popular kids, the social outcasts, and everyone in between, just like there were in your own school days.

That's great—it gives you a frame of reference and helps you understand your child's experience. But make no mistake, your kids' new, always-on, always-connected world presents some significant differences. Layer on issues such as exclusion, conflict, and online cruelty, and you can see why today's parents are filled with anxiety. I see it every day in my practice.

Same Stuff, Different (Digital) Environment

Today's kids hang out via social media instead of stoops, backyards, parking lots, and malls. Did you grow up in a city, a suburb, or a rural area? Where did you congregate with your friends? In ninth grade, my friends and I found an unused bathroom off the high school theater. We ate lunch there, skipping the throngs in the cafeteria and claiming some space of our own. Kids seek out places to be with their peers away from the watchful eyes of adults.

Now, social media and online games are prime gathering places. Simply using—and being seen using—group texts or certain social apps is one way many kids try to fit in. They may be socializing with their friends or with a wider peer group, and not only is every group dynamic different, but they change all the time. Also, the rules of engagement are seemingly set by some and followed by others.

Your kid may be participating in a group text but still feel left out, while another kid might be blissfully unaware that anything is amiss. If you are a nonconformist in middle school, it is probably easiest if you are so "out there" that you truly don't care what other kids think. But from what I observe of middle schoolers, that is pretty unusual! Just like you remember from your time in school, having a "tribe" of fellow nonconformists can help—this can be just one or two friends to sit with at lunch or do other things with.

Social Differences from Analog to Digital

Previous generations likely had greater independent range and more unstructured time than our kids have today. That affected how involved our friendships were, and how we worked out conflicts and power struggles. Also, consider that you may have a very different personality than your child—perhaps your family moved all the time and you had to develop a repertoire of friend-making skills, while your child has had the same best friend from preschool to the present. One change from our own childhoods is that the school gossip and drama can reach kids more easily via text messages and social media.

Thus, you may want to consider—especially if your child experiences social drama as a negative factor in her life—helping her plug into another community. There are many places to connect with kids outside of school: scouts, a youth group through your religious community, classes or clubs offered through local parks and recreation departments or community groups, and so on. My own experience of this gave me great perspective on the larger world. When I was in middle school, and not exactly the belle of the eighth-grade ball, I joined a camera club that had mostly retired members. It was a completely different experience for me, and the members were very welcoming. Getting out of the bubble of other thirteen-year-olds was an unexpected bonus!

The work of growing up and figuring out who you are is complicated, and we don't want kids to "crowdsource" their identity in the digital realm. Obsessing over daily feedback and likes is a cycle that can only add to insecurity. You want to help your child stake her own claim to an identity and focus on being a good friend to those friends who are supportive and kind. This should extend from real-world interactions into online relationships, to social media and online games, too. The more negatively social media makes your kids feel, the more important it is that at least some after-school and evening time be "unplugged."

Differences from the "old days":

- You could hide out at home from drama at school.
- Adults were unlikely to see the drama and/or cruelty playing out between kids (this can still be true, though sometimes kids print a transcript or forward nasty comments).
- Kids could only compare themselves to people they knew locally (for many kids, the wider range of peers and potential role models is an advantage).

When Following Hurts

If your child follows someone on social media who consistently posts things that make your child feel left out, you might suggest that he unfollow that person for a week. A permanent disconnection or deletion of the app will probably feel too extreme to your child, but framing it as a *temporary measure* can help. Once your child sees that he feels better, he may decide to extend or maintain the disconnection.

Sometimes deleting the app (or just waiting to join a social space) is the best option. One fifth grader, Karina, told me that another girl had blocked her on an app. Getting blocked can be so painful, but it truly may be better than seeing everything that person shares. This girl was several years younger than the thirteen-and-up age guidelines most social apps advise, and Karina's early entry in this milieu was causing negative feelings that outweighed any benefit. This is a scenario that calls for for parental guidance—and probably dumping the app for a while.

Impact on Identity

Middle schoolers, in particular, are at a key point in their development. They are starting to form their own identity, trying on new personae and testing boundaries every day. If you have a sixth grader in the house right now, you know exactly what I'm talking about. While this search for identity is not new, it looks a little different when you layer social media over an already intense and complicated time.

Part of our role as parents is to talk to our kids about what to share, and about the choices we all make about when to conform or when to resist conformity.

Some kids start out independent but become more conformist in middle school as a way to survive the sometimes harsh social winnowing that can occur. Other kids have been trying to fit in forever and tend to follow the crowd. As best you can, resist your own judgment about your child's conformity (or nonconformity), and instead help her to see it for herself. You want your child to feel confident about her choices. As parents, we can agree that we don't want our daughters to give up ice hockey if they love it, just because a lot of their female friends are gravitating to gymnastics. On the other hand, if your daughter then wants the exact same headband that her friends have, resist judgment there, too.

Ira Glass, host of the popular documentary radio show *This American Life*, interviewed three high school freshman girls (two fourteen-year-olds and one fifteen-year-old) about how the comments on photos they share reinforce their friendships.[1] This is worth noting not because these rules are universal, but so we can understand that the group our children circulate in, whatever that group is, has some rules.

For example, the girls said that commenting on someone's photo can be a way to get to know that person, or let him or her know you might like to be friends: "Especially because we, like, just started high school, so we're meeting a lot of new people. So you would comment on someone's photo who you're not really super close with or that you don't know really well. And it's sort of a statement, like, I want to be friends with you, or I want to get to know you, or like, I think you're cool."[2]

The girls also discussed the importance of reciprocity; if you get a comment, you may be expected to comment on one of the commenter's photographs. When close friends don't comment on a shared photo, the girls pointed out: "You definitely feel insecure. Because, like, you expect them to comment, and they don't, and you're like, why?" One girl, Jane, described how a "non-response" can feel like a snub: "Like, what if they've seen it and they're just not liking it on purpose, or like, what if everybody who's seeing it thinks that we're not actually friends because they're not commenting on it. They haven't commented yet. It's been X amount of time and they still haven't liked it."

All of the girls acknowledged that they haven't asked for responses and it "seems kind of shallow" to expect comments all the time, but they also feel obligated to keep up with the shared expectation.

While the girls mention that their parents think that intense focus on comments is a waste of time, parents would do well to empathize with kids' need for positive reinforcement at this age. The possibilities for constant feedback, combined with the challenges of this stage of adolescence, can create an irresistible cycle. But the cycle often leaves kids hungry for more, no matter how many comments they get. For parents, maintaining a sense of humor and perspective about teenagers' rituals is helpful. The girls seem to understand their parents' skepticism here, which is a nice thing about teenagers. While a nine-year-old might be hurt that parents think something they care about is stupid, a fourteen-year-old is often able to see both perspectives and to have a sense of humor about her own intense need to get and give responses. Cultivating that distance and perspective is part of growing up. One of the girls, Ella, quotes her mother as saying: "Why is everyone doing this? Like, why are fifty people feeling the need to tell you that you're pretty?" And Julia believes her dad thinks "it's kind of stupid."

Friends Versus Followers

The concept of "friend" has been somewhat redefined by social media. Whether we like it or not, the world of social media has altered the concept a little, and it's worth understanding the difference so that we can help our kids understand it too. There's no doubt that today's online friendships add challenges to the social sphere—as if it weren't complicated enough!

Today's kids are dealing with a bigger public than we did. There are two sides to "the public": (1) the public made up of the people they know personally and (2) the wider world of those who happen to see their public posts.

One of the ever-present questions around social media, whether you've been using it for years or are just starting out, is the size of your audience and whom it includes. Each ecosystem around each user is unique, like a fingerprint. Anyone who uses a social platform has a universe of friends or followers, and those who use more than one platform may have multiple universes. These universes may be very small or quite large. In open platforms like Twitter, audiences can grow to numbers that are hard to fathom, and there's no way you'd know all your followers personally.

Many adults can relate to the experience of feeling like they had to connect with everyone and anyone who asked in the early days of Facebook. Even now, if a colleague or another person you know professionally wants to friend you, it can be awkward to refuse. Clear boundaries—such as "I don't friend people from work"—can be helpful.

Firm boundaries are especially necessary for younger kids. For instance, maybe you don't allow them to friend people you (the parents) don't know. When you are talking with younger kids about expected peer/friend behavior, depending on how socially sophisticated your kids are, talk about the idea of close friends versus a wider circle. It's worth doing this even before they are on social media. Talk to them about what makes a good friend, or ask them about an existing friend and the reasons she's a good friend.

In my workshops with third graders, I often ask what makes a good friend. You may remember from chapter 3 that they say, "someone who's kind," "someone you have fun with," "someone who shares," "someone who isn't mean," or "someone who feels good to hang out with." Not surprisingly, when I ask them about what makes a person good to play games with, their answers are similar. They like a friend who "doesn't get angry too easily," "doesn't cheat," or "doesn't want to quit playing when they aren't winning." Just opening up this conversation can lead to an understanding about establishing boundaries.

The goal here is to make an understanding of friendship part of their value set rather than a pattern of behavior that's attached to a particular platform or to social media in general. It's not mere etiquette or social media management; it's a part of their core values. That's digital citizenship.

Establishing the Difference Between Types of Friends

Teaching our kids about the difference between real friends and our "social media public" is important. What are the criteria for each category? How do you know the difference? Can you be friends with someone you've never met in person or talked to on the phone? Can a follower become a friend?

Start out by putting some simple limits in place. If your child is new to social media, start her with some digital training wheels. Maybe you can assert that you only want your son to follow people he knows already. You could even stipulate that it is important that *you* know them too, if you have concerns. Maybe this won't be a permanent rule, but you can start out this way. Have your child set his account to "private," and he will be required to approve each follow request.

Privacy settings and policies change so often in the world of social media platforms that there is little specific advice I can provide here that will be lasting. It helps to use strategies, like having your child show you other kids' accounts that are positive or negative, that will endure no matter what changes are made to the platform itself. App-specific tactics are only helpful as long as that app is around—or until the app changes its settings! One technique I use is to enter "privacy settings APPNAME 20__(current year)" into my favorite search engine to find recent articles about privacy issues or updates. When Snapchat was hacked in 2015, forty-six million users found out the hard way that social media isn't a good place to share your most private images and updates.

Romance and Crushes in the Digital Age

The Pew Research Center's Internet and American Life Project is one of my favorite sources for useful data on the ways kids and families use technology. In October 2015, the center released a study showing that (surprise!) kids are still falling in love, getting crushes, getting mad, getting even, etc.[3] So things haven't changed...that much. But for those parents who worry about the complications that technology brings to dating life, I have some good news: at least in 2015, most kids were not actually meeting or "hooking up" with other people online.

It may feel like dating has moved entirely to the Internet, but according to the same Pew study, only 8 percent of American teens have met a romantic partner online.[4] Though we see a few young people using Tinder, Grindr, and other "hookup" apps, these are supposed to be used only by those eighteen or older. Also, as one mother of a ninth grader told me, despite the racy implications of such apps, her son Alex started a traditional dating relationship with a girl, Talia, he met via Tinder. In this day and age, "traditional" means that Alex's mother drove her son to a bookstore café to meet Talia in person for the first time while she waited outside. Since then, Alex's mother has met Talia's parents, and the families have gotten together to go to the kids' basketball games and school plays. While Alex and Talia live twenty minutes apart in different suburbs—and may not have otherwise met—their relationship itself does not seem any different than if they had met at a swim meet or debate tournament.

For gay, lesbian, bisexual, transgender, and questioning kids, social media and the Internet can be incredibly positive sources of validation, information, and community. They can also be sites for bullying, so adults need to be aware of this possibility. For young people trying to navigate different identities in different situations (e.g., kids who are out in some settings, but not in others) social media presents many complications. Here are some great resources for these kids and their families: http://www.safeschoolscoalition.org/, http://www.glsen.org/and http://www.impactprogram.org/lgbtq-youth/youth-blog/ as well as the book I mentioned in chapter 5, *This Is a Book for Parents of Gay Kids*. All kids need age appropriate information about sexuality, bodies, and sexual health, as well.

Expectations Change with Constant Connectivity

Once teens or tweens are involved romantically, their expectations are surely affected by the availability of constant connection. This is parallel to the changes in expectations we face in our own adult relationships. For example, my husband and I were dating before we had cell phones, yet today our expectations for being in contact (while far lower than those of teenagers!) are higher than they were before we had these devices with us at all times. Fully 85 percent of young people surveyed expected to hear from their partner at least once a day. Eleven percent expected to hear from their partners once an hour![5]

Teens are just getting used to the physical and emotional changes that come with puberty, and one of those is the infatuation with others their age. While in the past, flirtatious exchanges may have been confined to lunch and the occasional movie, today every couple can keep in never-ending contact via their phones. When talking to your child, remind her that the fact that she can reach out to her crush at all times does not mean she has to. It's okay not to text.

On the other hand, flirting, dropping hints, and trying to figure out how mutual an interest is (age-old preoccupations) have moved more into the digital realm. In the Pew study, 50 percent of teens reported that they used Facebook or other social media platforms to flirt or express romantic intentions.[6] While kids may still prefer to meet romantic partners at school or through friends, social media is often where they feel most comfortable discussing their feelings.

Kids can be clumsy, inept, and immature about relationships. After all, they are kids! In one of my focus groups, a girl described how boys badgered her with repeated texts until she texted back. Then one boy erased the previous texts to make it look as if the girl texted first, so he could show his friends, "Look, she texted me!" Kids on either end of this exchange might benefit from adult mentorship, or they may figure it out on their own by trial and error.

Think about how you might mentor your child—on either end of the texting exchange where the boy badgered the girl into texting him. Ask your kids: What are the most annoying things other kids do in these digital spaces? And how do kids deal with those things when they happen? One parent pointed out that marry/kiss/kill can also be an in-person game. Digital connections just make it easier for answers to be shared widely. Talk with your children about the possible outcomes when people text or post messages intended to be kept between friends. Is that intent always honored? Ask your child if she has ever seen someone share a screenshot of someone's personal texts. Why do people do it? Is it ever okay? How can you protect yourself, knowing that this is technically possible, and in fact happens frequently?

Dealing with Unwanted Attention

In addition to meeting and starting romantic relationships, kids are negotiating breakups and fending off unwanted attention in both the traditional ways (face to face and talking on the phone) and the digital realm (social media, texting, e-mail). The Pew study reports that 25 percent of all teens have unfriended or blocked someone on social media because that person was flirting in a way that made them uncomfortable.[7] Perhaps, not surprisingly, teen girls are more likely to be the recipients of uncomfortable online flirting, with 35 percent reporting they've unfriended or blocked someone, more than twice as many as the 16 percent of boys who have done the same.[8]

One way to open the door to conversations about these kinds of experiences is to ask your child if she or her friends have ever had to block someone for coming on too strong or being too persistent. Make sure she knows that aggressive behavior is unacceptable and that she doesn't have to put up with it. If the behavior doesn't stop when she unfriends or blocks the perpetrator, you may need to contact the school—or the authorities.

Harassment can take many forms. One form could be sharing a sexual story (whether true, sort of true, or completely made up) about another person.

A mother at one of my parent talks told me that her daughter left a messenger app open on her phone. She saw that her daughter had texted a boy after a recent overnight youth group event at their synagogue, saying, "I can't believe you told everyone we @#$#ed, I would never go near you and you know it!" In the back-and-forth texting, the boy apologized and the girl said, "Never lie about me again." In the end, they seemed to have made up with a mutual,

"Okay, we're cool now." Rather than confronting her daughter or even bringing up the situation, the mother felt proud that her daughter stuck up for herself. She noted to herself that the kids in her daughter's age cohort were at least talking about sex, and made sure to check in more about sex and relationships with her daughter, though she never brought up the situation.

While girls may be more likely to face harassment or feel that they have to block aggressive "flirting," I should point out that over-enthusiastic pursuit definitely goes both ways. Numerous parents have told me that their sons get a ton of calls or texts from girls and sometimes do not know how to deal with that. Especially in fifth to seventh grade, girls may be interested in boys at a time when boys are not ready yet. Learning to deal with someone who does not reciprocate your feelings is a major milestone of growing up and learning about love and dating. The wider social sphere can make the interactions more nuanced, so it's up to us as parents to help our kids by guiding them and setting boundaries as necessary.

One boy's parents recounted a conversation they'd had with another child's parents: "I told the girl's parents that she is texting my son thirty to forty times a day, at all hours, but they don't do anything about it." Clearly, this is a situation crying out for boundaries. A younger boy may not know how to respond, or may respond in a cruel or embarrassing way (e.g., sharing the texts with everyone). Think about it—that would only make a bad situation worse. Another mother told me that her daughter received a very mean text response from a boy she had a crush on. When she told the boy's mother (they already knew one another) the mother blew it off, leaving the girl's mother surprised and disappointed.

If other parents approach you about your child's behavior, try not to be defensive. Thank them for coming to you first, and let them know you'll look into it—then report back to resolve the problem.

Working with other parents, you can help guide and mentor your kids. Mentorship seeks to build communities, not form divisions. The more we know about our kids and their peer groups, the better we can help them navigate their world as competent and fully realized digital citizens.

Technology Is Functional, People Are Emotional

Texting can feel like a great way to stay in touch with friends, but it also has some pitfalls. It's great for quick exchanges and making plans. For many adults, the best uses of texting are functional and practical. Emotional issues, on the other hand, don't translate well in text messages or social media. They are too complex for such simple media. We can talk with kids about sticking with the functional aspects, but the reality is, if the relationships are happening via text, then the intense stuff and the feelings will be there too. Talk with your kids about different situations that can arise via text so they get a feel for what's appropriate and what's not.

Kids also need to exhibit patience when friends are not responsive. There is nothing more annoying than coming back to your phone and finding twenty messages from someone who just couldn't deal with the fact that you were eating dinner or doing homework. These could be messages from within an application or traditional text messages. Help your kids imagine what their friends are doing and set boundaries for their friends so they don't feel anxious about what they might be missing.

This same issue can surface in online games. Jonathan, my fifth-grade Minecraft expert, pointed out that sometimes he is away from the game, but his laptop is still open to Minecraft. In other words, it appears that he's still playing, even though he's not.

And when a player doesn't respond right away, hurt feelings can result. Even though Jonathan understands the issue ("You might not even be right by your computer"), his friends sometimes misunderstand a non-response as a willful snub. One solution is to teach kids to close out of the game, so others know they are not active at the moment.

Texting and communicating are important parts of kids' social sphere, so invest time in helping them learn the unwritten rules. In my experience working with kids, they are often eager to have a space to discuss the challenges that texting can bring. Here are some questions to ask your child about texting. In some cases, asking a group of kids to engage on this topic may provoke more discussion than a one-on-one talk with your child.

- What is fun—and not fun—about group texting?
- Have any of your friends ever texted too much or too many times?
- What should you do if you text someone and he doesn't text back right away?
- Have any of your friends ever showed your texts to someone else?

Try to be calm and nonreactive, and let your child describe his experience.

Exclusion in Social Media

Whether intentionally or not, kids exclude other kids. In real-world social spaces, this is complicated to manage. In the digital world, the dynamics are even more complex.

Every social media workshop I do with kids offers them room to talk about one of the major problems that social media can exacerbate—the feeling that everyone is hanging out and having fun without you. It is one thing to learn about something you missed after the fact; it is even more painful to watch photos posted in real time by kids who are at a party or get-together that is taking place without you. Kids in my workshops say it is especially hurtful to see such social posts if a friend has lied to them—but even if a friend said openly that she couldn't hang out because she had "other plans," they may feel bad if they see those other plans that don't include them. Even seeing kids with their families can make us feel left out. Why? People rarely document disagreements or the kids fighting in the backseat—they are more likely to share the one blissful moment, or at least the one moment that everyone is smiling for the camera. Social media tends to show the positive views of life (which is good), but it can set a standard that's impossible to live up to.

The Performative Nature of Social Media

In addition to making us feel that we are missing out on specific experiences, social media can lead us to feel like our whole mood or approach to life is wrong if we are not constantly winning, smiling, or having an epic moment. One of the most important things adults can offer kids in our "connected" times is the information that social media has a strong performative element. People are sharing only pieces of themselves, sometimes in a calculated way and sometimes in a thoughtless way.

As parents, we need to get really curious about what it is like to be a young teen or tween with a smartphone. What's it like to be a sixth grader watching a slumber party you weren't invited to unfold on social media in real time while you are at home on a Saturday night? Is it better as a tenth grader because you're more self-secure? Or is it worse, because you see several different things you were excluded from? As kids get older, they may become better at coping, but for some kids, high school and even college may feel like a series of social events they are missing out on.

Talk with your children about the ways people perform happiness and social connection on social media, and explain that such posts sometimes cover up feelings of sadness, self-doubt, and insecurity. After University of Pennsylvania student Madison Holleran committed suicide, her friends considered the happy image they had all created of sailing through their first year of college, even though, privately, each of them struggled with the transition. In a moving article, "Madison Holleran's Friends Share Their Unfiltered Life Stories,"[9] each of Holleran's surviving close friends shared how they were really feeling in a happy-looking photo they'd posted on Instagram. This is a great article to share with high school–aged kids about the ways social media can feel like a space we have to perform in.

What Can You Do to Help?

To help your children feel less alone, share your own experiences of feeling excluded. Encourage kids who are feeling excluded to take a little social media "vacation". Especially if your child is in transition between groups of friends or has recently ended a friendship, too much time focusing on "ex-friends" can be a problem. This is also true for romantic and dating relationships (see more later in this chapter). Your child may be tempted to spend hours following his former sweetie on social media, and we need to teach an alternative to this painful and damaging behavior.

It also helps kids to know that they can block certain people, or use parents as an excuse to spend less time on social media. It really is better not to know that everyone is hanging out without you, and that sometimes they are even trying to make you feel bad by letting you know. Ouch.

These are some good conversation starters for talking with your child about social media:

- Do you think some kids feel left out on social media (or group texts)?
- Describe a time that you felt left out because of something you saw on Instagram.
- Describe a time that you thought about not posting something because you worried that other people might feel left out.
- What are some things you can do if you are looking at Instagram and you feel like you are missing out on something?
- Do you ever feel that if you take a break from your phone you might miss something really important?
- Do you think people ever purposefully post pictures of themselves having fun with friends to make others feel left out?
- What might someone get from doing such a thing?

One group of middle schoolers I worked with responded this way to a question about how you can help yourself feel better when you are excluded:

- Watch a movie
- Eat some ice cream
- Call some other friends to invite them over
- Don't watch—put away your phone!
- Exercise
- Hang out with your family

These kids were able to admit that if they had other friends over, they might be tempted to take and share pictures. When I asked why she would share pictures at all, one girl said that she wants to "show that she has a life outside of school." Another kid said, "It is fun to share when you are doing fun things." Other kids pointed out that social media is a way to mark the moment and preserve memories.

I asked the kids, "Do you think people just shouldn't share images of events that exclude people?," and they all said, "No! People have a right to share." One girl clarified that "one is okay, two is a bit much, and three or more pics from the same event starts to be obnoxious." As I have described elsewhere, the rules are different in different regions and contexts, but kids are defining the social rules in their communities.

Putting the phone away is one great idea these middle schoolers identified. Tell your child that making a choice not to ruminate over your exclusion is a huge step toward empowerment.

Conflict (and Repair)

While technology itself is not usually the root cause of teen or tween angst, it can certainly exacerbate a problem. If we understand the digital world to be a parallel world, then we can see that each problem would exist in the analog, face-to-face world as well. But when you put the problems in a digital environment, you can see them get more complicated—or at least you can see added layers of complexity.

In my student workshops, I ask kids to brainstorm about how to correct mistakes they make in the digital realm. A common problem is an "overshare," where they have shared something too personal about themselves. Another is when they share a friend's good news, or even a secret.

Kids know they can't put the overshare or secret "back in the box," but their instincts are to try to limit the damage. Quickly. In these workshops, they suggest taking down the offending post or deleting the picture and apologizing, or at least letting people know that it was a mistake.

But how can they make it right? In many settings, from youth groups to religious schools to public schools, I hear proposed solutions that are themselves troubling. For instance, many kids will try to "spread some lies" to cover a truth they've shared. Another is allowing revenge: "I'll let my friend spread a rumor about me," for example. Embroiled in a social error, kids may feel an urgency to take further steps to fix it "for good," all at once.

These problem-solving techniques came from fifth and sixth graders who are just learning to negotiate complicated social relationships. Many of these kids are getting their first communication device, which adds a layer of complexity to the equation.

We have to help kids understand that rumors, lies, and revenge strategies only exacerbate a bad situation. Kids are focused on the immediate issue and often have trouble seeing the larger picture. Sometimes, when the parameters of trust in a relationship change, it takes time to fix—and your child can actually make matters worse by trying to fix the breach of trust in one gesture.

It is especially important for kids to be aware that it can be hard to repair an emotionally charged situation without communicating in person. Choosing a communication medium wisely and not out of fear is part of the skill set of conflict resolution.[10] We have to let kids know that when we get an e-mail or text that upsets us, we take time to take a breath. Then, if possible, we talk with the person face to face or at least by phone. Think of times when an e-mail at work left you with steam coming out of your ears, but you were able to diffuse the situation through a face-to-face conversation or just a sympathetic look and the question, *do you want to talk?*

Talk to your kids, too, about what to do when they are recruited into other people's conflicts. What do they do if they see a nasty exchange as part of a group text or a rude comment on someone's picture? Sometimes we avoid conflict ourselves but get involved emotionally in other people's conflicts. If your child finds himself witnessing or being drawn into such a conflict, he can say that he feels uncomfortable with the conversation and he can get out or make an excuse to get out; he might also contact the target of the mean behavior to say he is sorry that this happened. Make sure your child knows that if the behavior is serious or threatening, he should report it to a parent, a teacher, or another responsible adult.

We all make mistakes. Kids need to see that relationships are complex, even for adults. It's important that they learn how to manage mistakes with honesty, empathy, and patience. How can you model the idea of relationship repair? Can you offer a personal story of a communication gone wrong and how you solved it? The following story of relationship repair came from a parent at one of my workshops: "I thought everyone knew Aunt Marcy was expecting a baby, and so I said something about it on Facebook. She had every right to be mad at me—it wasn't my news to share. I should have checked with her about how public her news was before I assumed. I called her to apologize—I feel really bad about it, but we had a good conversation, and I certainly won't do something like that ever again."

Patience is the toughest thing to teach to our digital natives. Speed of communication is a virtue in today's world, but it heightens the sense of urgency. Kids feel like they have to resolve things quickly,[11] which we can understand. No one wants to feel the stress of a difficult relationship. But repair is not always fast. It can take time. Teach your kids that it's okay to take time and gain perspective. Mistakes present an opportunity to teach children good life skills in general. Owning up to your missteps, apologizing earnestly, and returning to being a good friend are the best ways to move past any issue.[12]

Another challenge of relating in digital spaces is the way missteps are public within the peer and friend groups. A common worry I see among parents of middle schoolers is that a misstep will lead to embarrassment in the larger public, something "the whole school might see." In reality, it is the micro-peer group misstep that is much more likely to give your child nightmares. Trying to be funny in a group text when everyone takes it the wrong way, commenting on someone else's photo and hitting the wrong note, or even posting something and not getting likes or comments can all be humiliating and isolating for kids. As one teenager, Jane, pointed out when she was interviewed on *This American Life*, kids who are very involved in social media see it as a way of "mapping out your social world, seeing who's with who, who's hanging out with who, who is best friends with who."[13] And those revelations can be painful.

One thing I tell parents before their kids get their first device is that social media is going to turn up the dial on whatever is happening. It won't make your introverted kid more extroverted. It won't make a kid who is confident and secure into a bully or the target of a bully. However, it may turn up the volume on intergroup struggles for power, feelings of exclusion, and other social dilemmas. Social media tends to amplify issues between friends, sometimes escalating minor conflicts to major skirmishes.

Tech-Based Amplification of Problems

Conflicts are inevitable in any social sphere. And when they do occur, social media is unlikely to help matters. As I say, "When in doubt, take it offline." It is especially important to teach kids the skills to mend fences in person. When they are trying to resolve a dispute, a sense of urgency can take over and the conflict can escalate quickly. Ask your child to think of examples when it is better to exercise restraint, be patient, and resolve problems in a face-to-face discussion. The phone can work, too, but it's extremely difficult to resolve an argument via text message. Suggest to your child that he can avoid escalating a conflict with a simple message, such as, "Texting might not be the best way to discuss this—can we talk F2F?"

Even a nonresponse can be misinterpreted. We teach our kids to have good boundaries and let their friends know when they can't respond, but that doesn't mean their friends won't panic. In one of my focus groups, a popular and athletic twelve-year-old girl with a huge group of friends said: "People think you are mad at them when you don't respond right away. They text 'are u mad at me?' You can tell them I wasn't mad; I just wanted to be off my phone. I read your message but I didn't have time to respond."

The kids pointed out that in many programs you can tell if someone has read your message. If the friend hasn't read your text, it is easier to manage impatience…but if she *has* read it, a kid might wonder what on earth could prevent a response. To help your kids gain skills in handling such delays, model patience and understanding, and even talk yourself through your emotions so that your kids can hear you. For example, you could say: "I texted Dad and I really want to know his plans so we can buy these plane tickets. It is hard to wait, but I bet he's talking to his boss or a client right now. I am going to work on something else so I don't get tempted to bug him." Conflicts can be intense when they are so easily shared with a drama-loving audience of peers. This is another area where communicating in the digital realm is akin to pouring gasoline on a fire. Tweens and teens may be all too eager to jump in on someone else's conflict. Ask your child if she has ever felt "recruited" into other people's conflicts. What if a nasty exchange erupts as part of a group text, or someone posts a rude comment on someone else's Instagram picture? Do you get involved? Will that help, or could it make matters worse? As I often say, conflict can be a spectator sport.

One seventh-grade girl in one of my focus groups described social media conflict starting from the comments on shared photos: "There were too many sides and they try to draw you in stupid fights for stupid reasons. I try not to get involved, then people will get mad at me. Then it gets more complicated . . ."

If you have a middle schooler (or an upper elementary schooler), let your child know he can always use you as an excuse. If a group text is going in a negative direction, talking in mean ways about another child (or a teacher, or anyone, really), your child should feel he can say, "My dad looks at my phone, I've got to bounce." Or, "I will get in big trouble if I am part of this." He can also just take a stand and say, "This is getting mean, I'm out." But sometimes the parent excuse is very helpful.

In *Odd Girl Out,* her study of relational aggression between girls, Rachel Simmons gives an example of a texted conversation between two girls in which one girl not so subtly recruits the other to "ice out" a third girl. The veneer of friendship can be a cover for the intense relational aggression that Simmons and others have documented. This kind of aggression is not limited to girls. As Simmons has described, boys also experience and fear relational aggression, even though we sometimes imagine boys' interactions to be more straightforward, with the aggression between them being more physical and overt.[14]

Both boys and girls can be subtly aggressive via texting or social media. The ability to replay those texts or comments, looking at them again and again, is a one of the downsides of communication in the digital realm. The ease of sharing ("Would you look at this text—I can't believe she said that about you") is another. It is now easy to record other people and share what they've said out of context. In her TED Talk, "The Price of Shame," Monica Lewinsky describes the excruciating experience of hearing her phone conversations with her (supposed) friend, knowing that they had been made public.[15] I think that this is an experience anyone can relate to. Even if you haven't encountered it firsthand, imagine a conversation in which you've openly discussed something intensely personal, and then imagine that the conversation was recorded and shared. It's a huge breach of trust. Thankfully, most of our children won't have conversations of high public interest recorded, as Lewinsky did. But just one text message shown out of context can mimic the effect, and can feel like a major betrayal.

More Serious Issues: Online Cruelty

Understanding your child's role in her social world will help you know what you need to be concerned about. Is your child in demand enough socially that there are kids "following" her every move—and potentially feeling left out because of it? Is she "following" a kid or two or three who barely know she exists? Is he on group texts because he wants to participate or because he worries about what others might say if he's not a part of the conversation? Helping your child set healthy boundaries around social media will go a long way toward helping him survive adolescence with self-esteem and a strong sense of his own identity.

By the time social media comes into the picture for your child, you may already have a sense of where he fits into the social mix. Is your son an alpha kid, liked or feared by everyone? Is your daughter socially vulnerable and more of a "people pleaser"? Or maybe your son is a confident introvert with one or two good friends? Orient yourself to your child's space, boundaries, models, and influencers. Learn all you can by observing for yourself, holding your judgment at bay. This is the way to gain a deeper understanding of your child's world, which is critical if you are going to offer sound guidance and support.

Once you understand your kid's social position, ask him to share with you his perspective on other kids' social media self-presentation. If he wants to use an app, can he show you how other kids use the app? You can often see quite a bit of an app even if you are not an account holder. Your child's critiques of his peers' accounts will tell you a lot! You can ask him if he has ever been surprised by what someone was like in person if he saw that person on social media before they met.

When bullying or other bad behavior comes up, things get more sensitive and emotionally charged. Ask your kid to distinguish bullying from more typical conflicts or drama. Does your child know the boundaries? Does he have a sense of when things have gone too far? Does he feel safe going to school? Would he tell you if something was out of control? Having a good sense of these things will put you in a much better position should something truly serious come up.

Certain indicators can help you decide when you, as a parent, should be concerned about your child's behavior in his digital world. For instance, do you see your child enjoying the drama and thriving in the chaos of conflict? This is a sure sign of a problem, and indicates that it is time for you to step in as a mentor. But if the drama is isolating or upsetting your child, you need to be even more proactive in helping him create boundaries. A kid who is too absorbed in the lives of others via social media needs to be actively guided toward other pursuits. Otherwise, the voyeur position can lead to negative feelings and behaviors. Social media is inherently a bit voyeuristic, so viewing habits are only concerning if they seem obsessive or are making your child stressed, withdrawn, or depressed.

Following are some examples of digital drama that may or may not lead to bullying or other forms of online cruelty. As isolated or reciprocal events, these may not fall into the bullying category, but taken to an extreme they certainly could:

- Taking other kids' phones and sending out mean, stupid, or silly text messages from the swiped phone (look out, it can happen fast!).
- Sharing embarrassing pictures of another kid. The range is huge here; look for severity of the image or continued behavior as indicators of harassment/bullying.
- Starting anonymous rumors (same as above).
- Trying to instigate trouble between two other friends.
- "Innocently" pointing out that someone unfollowed another.
- Stirring up conflict via comments on a social media site, also known as "trolling."
- Making oblique references on a group text to someone who "shouldn't really be on this group text."

Ask your child if she has seen other kids being mean in these spaces. As a parent, you will absolutely want to seek help if your child is afraid or too embarrassed to go to school, can't sleep, or is extremely distressed by some of the above scenarios. On the other hand, as much as possible, try to keep an open mind about what role your child might have played in the situation. It's natural to jump to your child's defense. But "fighting fire with fire" rarely works in an online space because the field is very wide. Emphasize to your child that if she feels attacked, she cannot retaliate online without it coming back to her. Also emphasize that threats or meanness should be documented—and then she should leave the app. There's no need to hang out there and continue to be victimized. Tell her to get immediately to safety in the company of parents or other trusted adults or friends. Then she can problem-solve with the adults and figure out how to handle the situation.

Assessing Your Kids' Social Skills

I hope that this chapter has given you a good overview of your child's peer-to-peer social world. While it's not significantly different in spirit from the world we remember from our own school days, it certainly has a lot more layers to it.

Here's a brief set of criteria to help you do a social skills assessment:

- Can your child articulate the difference between a friend and a follower?
- Does she understand that she doesn't have to friend someone back if she doesn't want to?

- Does he know how to self-govern his texting activity?
- Can she handle unwanted attention in a clear and direct fashion?
- Does he come to you when a peer conflict crosses the line?
- Can she politely excuse herself from a group text or interaction?
- Can she tell you about a time she resisted posting something because of the way it might make someone feel?
- Can he point out to you examples of purposeful exclusion in his social sphere?
- Does she know how to "take it offline" early in the conflict, or does she leave it to others to do it?

Remember, you are there to help your kids navigate their world. As I always say, while they have the tech savvy, you have wisdom, which offers an immensely valuable compass by which to guide your child through treacherous social waters.

CHAPTER 8

School Life in the Digital Age

The school experience for today's kids is both similar to and different from what we as parents experienced when we were in school. On one hand, school is still a learning community with classmates, teachers, and principals. You still have show-and-tell, recess, nightly homework, pop quizzes, and standardized testing. There is still a school smell and a lunchbox smell that will take you back to your own school days.

But school has changed, too, and it can be hard to separate the impact of technology from other changes—increased homework, a greater emphasis on testing, changes to curricula, etc. As I mentioned in the chapter on friendship, your children's peer groups from school may be more accessible (virtually) on evenings and weekends.

Many schools have implemented 1:1 programs (sometimes written as one-to-one), through which every student is issued a tablet or a laptop. Student access to computers often has an effect on expectations surrounding homework and on the nature of parent–teacher communication. Some schools have innovative maker spaces that go beyond anything we experienced in yesterday's schools. And, of course, technology programs vary widely from school to school.

With all these changes, one of the biggest challenges of the digital age is distraction. I hear this issue come up over and over again from parents and teachers. Parents hear that kids are gaming or surfing the web in class, and they are frontline witnesses to kids' distractions at home as they attempt to do their homework on tablets and laptops, sometimes with their phones in their hands as well.

Our access to information has transformed the way we relate to school as well. Communication and data flow back and forth much more freely and frequently, which has its advantages and challenges. Fliers that used to go home in backpacks have been supplanted by e-mail blasts, or even tweets in some schools. The possibility for increased access—communication between parents and teachers, between parents and their kids during the school day, and between students—is a change that both schools and parents are reckoning with, and often failing to acknowledge fully.

Many of the schools I work with bring me in to help administrators and staff understand the kinds of communication parents want, now that parents' expectations are being shaped by technology. As these norms and expectations shift, schools and school districts are hiring social media directors and communications experts. Even so, much of what you know about your child's day-to-day experience will come from his teacher. These are all real challenges that we'll be diving into in this chapter.

Assessing Your Relationship to Your Child's School

If you—or a group of parents—are thinking about how to deepen your understanding of your child's connected life at school, ask yourself the following questions:

- Are you informed about the school's practices with regard to technology? (Somewhat, not at all, totally)
- How do you handle digital distraction when it comes to homework? (Very well, it's a nightmare, depends on the night)
- Can you articulate to your child what constitutes original work?
- Are you an optimist or a cautionist when it comes to tech?
- Does your child prefer paper or e-books for her schoolwork?
- Do you know the stated expectations for parent–teacher communication?
- Since screen time is a blunt measure when your children may be studying and doing homework on devices, what is the best measure of technology use?
- Have you offered specific help to your child's school (or teacher) in the transition to 1:1?

Technology As a Distraction

At my school talks and other public events, parents frequently approach me with their concerns. In every community, technology as a distraction comes up as a frequent—and urgent—issue that worries parents.

Recent data from iKeepSafe suggests that parents are right to be concerned, with 28 percent of teens reporting that their digital engagement interferes with schoolwork.[1] Even outside the classroom, 44 percent of tweens admit that their digital pursuits take them away from other things they are doing, and 17 percent of tweens say that their digital engagement causes problems in relationships with friends and family.[2]

Adults are hardly exempt from such distractions (myself included!), with 14 percent of adults acknowledging that they need to spend less time with technology. If this issue is challenging for adults, imagine how difficult it is for kids. Teens and tweens are in need of mentorship to help them navigate these challenges. Let's face it, most of us aren't ready to unplug completely, as our digital engagement brings significant advantages. We shouldn't expect that our kids are willing to unplug either.

Kids who find that on-screen proofreading isn't very effective for a longer paper or a serious assignment should print their drafts and proofread them on paper. Going paperless sounds great, and it may be ecologically desirable, but many of us still may need to proofread our most important work on paper.

Homework and Distraction

Does this scene sound familiar? Your child goes to her room to complete her homework, perhaps on a school-issued iPad. Three hours later, she isn't finished. Was she perhaps iChatting or FaceTiming with her friends? Possibly, the talk started out about homework, but then the kids got pulled into other topics. Was your daughter listening to music and "had to" make a new playlist? Did she get distracted by a post on Instagram and feel she was missing out on a social "hangout" that very instant? Or was she just old-school daydreaming and not focusing?

Most kids in elementary and middle school shouldn't have three to four hours of homework. The homework epidemic is a topic for a whole different book, but do check with your child's teachers for guidelines about how much time they expect homework to take. If it's taking way too long (or not long enough), there may be an underlying problem.

Many kids need to unplug for homework. Again, check with

your child's teachers. Not all homework requires online time, so offline time during "home study hall" could be an effective tactic. Imagine the conversations with your spouse and the housework that would get done if you couldn't check your e-mail right after dinner!

Collaborating Against Distraction

If you observe that your children are struggling with distractions when completing homework on a tablet or laptop, collaborate with your kids to figure out how to tame the distractions. Here are some strategies—find the ones that are best for your family:

• **No double screening.** Many students I've spoken with say their parents have rules against double screening. Though this rule requires that kids have some willpower, have them put all but one device away. If a tablet is necessary to do homework, for instance, insist that they stick to that one device so they can focus.

• **Use tech to fight tech.** Some kids will appreciate and enjoy "distraction blockers" like LeechBlock and Freedom. While blocking won't solve the problem on its own, it can help! As I type this chapter, I am blocking social media myself. My friends' babies are cute and breaking news is exciting, but I need to focus.

• **Do homework in a common area of the home.** This works well for some families and is impractical for others.

• **Turn off the tech.** Many parents find that simply turning off their home Wi-Fi really helps kids get their work done. Again, the

Internet and connectivity are only small parts of most kids' homework. They may be expected to visit an interactive space to post a comment, but that is likely only a tiny portion of their homework. Even an assignment to write a blog post can be completed offline and posted later.

- **Start unplugged to get plugged-in.** If your kids say, "But I need to (collaborate with my friends, be online, use the Internet, etc.) to do my homework," have them complete all the non-Internet homework first and do the plugged-in homework last. Impose a time limit or be present yourself so they know that they need to finish.

- **Show your struggles too.** Finally, be open with your kids about your own experiences of distraction. Tell them your struggles—how distractions can be a drain on your productivity at work or that it feels tough to keep up with everything sometimes. Knowing this can be very helpful to them and make them feel like their own struggles are not abnormal.

Distraction is not just about the devices, but how we use them. Our devices add a lot to our lives, both positive and negative. Digital citizenship is about learning how to harness the positives and minimize the negatives. If you can get to the root cause of distraction, you will be in a much better position to mentor your kids to fight through it and get their homework done.

Multitasking and Distraction

I divide the research on kids and distraction into two broad categories: the optimists and the cautionists.

• **The optimists.** Techno-optimists believe our minds are getting stronger because of digital technology. Freed from having to remember a ton of facts, we can create and link ideas together in new and interesting ways. Professor Cathy Davidson argues that "monotasking" is not compatible with the way our brains work.[3]

• **The cautionists.** Techno-cautionists believe we are all in "the shallows,"[4] skimming and scanning and not truly reading. Indeed, before we all jump into e-textbooks, we should look at some of the evidence that format matters. Techno-cautionists are nervous about what we lose when we move away from printed books or handwritten notes. Some research and anecdotal experiences suggest that, when reading or taking notes, some learners may do better with paper than electronic devices.[5]

While there's more research to be done, some studies suggest that we retain information better when it's in paper form rather than digital form.[6] One question to keep in mind: Is this true only for people who already have a history of learning from paper texts? Or are there properties of printed text that affect memory, such as the physicality of turning a page and knowing where you are in a book? And how is this different for digital natives—our kids?

Larry Rosen, a psychology professor at California State University, Dominguez Hills, in research summarized by Annie Murphy Paul, found that groups of college students doing important homework checked their phones quite frequently.[7] We seek breaks in our work, and the mental work of toggling back and forth puts our best abilities at risk. While the actual interruption may seem to be only a few seconds, it takes us a while to reengage and get back into the flow of our work. This "dislocation" is a problem, as we may get fatigued from the effort of repeatedly bringing our minds back to a task. Thus, one hour of homework can take two or three hours and feel exhausting—but the effort is not from the work itself, but from the work of constantly refocusing.

As parents, we need to help our kids avoid double screening and to have a better grasp of the toll that toggling between tasks can take on our ability to work and think. As Alex Pang points out in *The Distraction Addiction*, "Digitally enabled switch-tasking tends to push several tasks into a narrow band of attention in a way that seems to short circuit your ability to really focus on what you need to do."[8] Pang points out that many of us overestimate the creativity and inspiration we get from switch-tasking and suggests that research shows instead that, "People who are heavy switch-taskers have a harder time than others concentrating for long periods."[9]

How Parent-Teacher Communication Has Changed

Technology has changed almost everything we do, and parent–teacher communication is no exception. You probably have more access to your child's teacher than you ever did, and certainly more than our parents had to ours. More access and more communication can be great things, but they come with some hazards, too. New modes of communication mean new etiquette and new expectations.

For instance, a common issue is expected response time. You reach out to the teacher, and you don't hear back right away. But how long is "right away," exactly? People's communication habits vary. You send another message. Now the situation has potentially escalated, when it really didn't have to.

Sometimes parents feel as though teachers are uneven in their grasp of new technology and in their use of it. In my experience, these differences are not as much about generation (I've seen many older teachers who are excited about opportunities to expand their personal learning network via Twitter, connect their students globally, and try new methods of collaboration) as they are about how well teachers are supported with professional development and whether they have the freedom to integrate technology in a way that makes sense. For some topics and certain students, teachers may wish to modify or transform the lessons using the tools of technology, or they may want to avoid using technology at all in instances where another method might be equivalent or better!

Parents (myself included) may struggle with organization as the volume of communication from school makes it hard to sort out the essentials. You may continue to get paper messages from some teachers, while others may use e-mail and yet others may use texts or tweets as reminders—and these varying modes of communication do create challenges for parents, for sure!

Here are some things parents can do to set a positive tone and foster good parent–teacher relationships.

1. **Teach boundaries to your child.** If your child is old enough to e-mail the teacher herself, then the child should also be aware and respectful of boundaries and expectations. Just because you and your child *can* e-mail the teacher doesn't mean it is a good idea in every case. Before you (or your child) e-mail the teacher, check whether the question can be resolved another way. If your child didn't write down the homework assignment, is it available from a classmate or via the learning management system? Your child should not make a habit of e-mailing the teacher instead of writing assignments down or looking them up. Remind yourself and your child that a teacher

who doesn't answer an e-mail right away may be in the middle of reading your child's essay, attending a professional development workshop, or eating dinner.

2. **Know the teacher's tools.** Is there a digital version of the textbook? Does the textbook—or the homework—require Internet access? If so, how much time will need to be spent on the Internet? These are great questions to ask the teacher, so you can mitigate distraction during homework time. If you know the basic parameters of the assignments, you can set up unplugged or partially plugged-in (computer or tablet not connected to Wi-Fi) time for homework.

3. **Adhere to school rules.** Don't make life difficult by sending your kid to school with devices when they are prohibited by the school. Despite your good intentions, prohibited devices will likely create a classroom issue. If you have a good reason, such as an urgent family matter or a particular health issue, ask the school to make an exception.

4. **Unfettered access to information is not always a good thing.** Lots of schools now let you check your child's grades on quizzes and tests as they are posted. Unless you are managing a particular struggle, this level of access to information may cause more stress than it is worth! The same goes for texting your kiddo during the day to "check in." If kids aren't supposed to be on their phones during school hours, don't make it hard for them to follow the rules.

Issues with 1:1 Programs

Moving to a 1:1 environment is a profound transition, which is no doubt why I receive many consulting requests every year to address it. Not only is the transition difficult for the school's teachers and administrators, it's also a big shift for parents. Let's say that 1:1 is coming to your child's school, and you have some questions. Often, the school will set up some events and online resources to address parents' concerns.

Despite their good intentions, schools and districts making this transition can be so busy with the transition itself that they don't always focus on parent communication and education. Parents want to feel informed and involved, and when schools don't ask for input from parents or respond to their questions in a thorough and timely way, parents may continue to raise concerns. Let's look at some of the issues that surface regularly.

1:1 at School

With the transition to 1:1 at schools, parents are often concerned about the increased screen time in their kids' lives. One question parents often ask is, "How does 1:1 affect the recommendation we always hear about limiting screen time?" First of all, 1:1 does not mean your child will be engaged with a tablet or laptop for his entire school day. But you can expect that your child will be engaged with the device at least one to two hours (cumulatively) most days, if not a bit more on some days.

Also, screen time may not be the most useful way to understand the varied ways we use technology. It might be better to think instead about balance—in other words, what kind of face-to-face collaboration and active engagement with the physical world is my child having? Is it enough to balance more sedentary learning, connecting, and even leisure time? Activities such as bike riding and building with clay may help balance math homework (whether on- or offline) or watching a video (whether for school or for fun).

Organizing and Managing Schoolwork

Sometime between third or fourth grade and high school, kids in many school systems are expected to move from simple nightly assignments into longer-term projects that require planning. The process of managing that planning, keeping track of materials and notes from school, and generally living an organized school life that doesn't involved wadded-up paper at the back of the locker or desk, lost homework, and tons of stress is called "executive function." Many students struggle with this, and, in my experience, expectations are not always realistic, leading students to outsource this executive functioning to parents. Teach kids to outsource to technology instead, which will be a great way for them to become what Howard Gardner calls "app enabled."[10] A great book for further help on this is Ana Homayoun's *That Crumpled Paper Was Due Last Week*.

Work with kids to review upcoming assignments against other plans before the due date—that is, we're travelling the weekend before that project is due, so you should have it almost finished by date ____. Looking at the calendar and working backward from deadlines is an advanced life skill, and few middle schoolers can do it on their own. Even learning to estimate how much time a task will take is pretty challenging. Learning to look at the calendar before making plans rather than trying to manage it all in your head is another challenge. The various high school babysitters my family uses seem to have a handle on this—few will commit without checking their calendars for availability. Many families find a physical calendar (dry erase or paper) to be essential. My own family relies on a digital calendar, but I can see that, as my son gets older, a physical representation in a central space at home will be helpful.

1:1 at Home

Many parents find that they need to make adjustments at home once a 1:1 school program comes into their child's life. Depending on how you use your own devices, it's easy to associate an iPad with leisure activities, even though your child really does need the device to do her homework. You may need to get a little more involved with your child's schoolwork, to help mitigate any potential issues. First, find out from your child's teacher not just how much time homework should take, but also when your child will need connectivity (if at all). Especially for group work, knowing the time window your child will need to be connected to her classmates can help.

Many parents want to supervise any time spent doing homework on a device, especially if that device is connected to the Internet. Having the child work at the kitchen table is a good strategy, but make sure that you provide her with a quiet work environment. Turn the TV off during that time and remove any other potential distractions. Doing this will get your child into good homework habits.

What if your child is "grounded" from technology? Can she still use her school device under supervision? Does it have to be disconnected from the Internet? Or can she be grounded from certain apps but not from the device itself? It is possible to restrict specific apps, if you are managing access via passwords. For many kids, being grounded from Minecraft or Instagram makes more sense than being device free. I would try not to publicly humiliate your child by forcing her to let her teacher know she is in trouble at home.

There is no question that if you take away your child's device and you let him use his school iPad or laptop with Internet access, he will find ways to chat with friends and he will feel like he is getting away with it. You have to decide how far you are willing to go to prevent that. If you turn off your home Wi-Fi for the weekend, are you willing to run to Starbucks to check your own e-mail? No one said having kids would be convenient! Of course, once your children have access to a 4G network on a smartphone, the whole picture changes!

Special Needs and 1:1

I've talked with numerous parents who have kids on 504 plans or IEPs (Individualized Education Programs) at school, as well as with special education teachers, about challenges that students with learning differences can have in a connected classroom. One mother told me that, for her son with high-functioning autism, the allure of choosing apps and swiping across the screen was simply too much for him to control. Another parent shared with me that her child with ADHD found some gaming a good way to manage the stress of school, but he was unable to control himself. In situations like these, working with the school and your child to figure out a way to grant some access but potentially lock down controls on his laptop or tablet could be part of a 504 plan or IEP. For some students, even slightly restricted access (e.g., checking the device in and out from certain teachers) works better than all-day access.

Work with the school to find ways to make this non-stigmatizing for your child. Your child may have her own suggestions. Many kids with ADHD or high-functioning autism respond very well to collaborative conversations about what would help them stay on task. There are also many excellent applications that can support kids with learning disabilities and spectrum and attention disorders, so the use of assistive technology and applications as part of a therapeutic program is well worth exploring.

On the other hand, while distraction presents significant challenges for kids with some neurological profiles, there are kids in school whose communication is enabled by technology along with skillful educators in a combination that is powerfully life changing for those students (and their families!). So the particular technology tools, the educational team's approach to technology, and the team's level of skill with your kid's specific profile are crucial.

Academic Dishonesty

Cheating has been around for as long as there have been schools, but there's little doubt that technology has amplified the problem. Tech-savvy kids can find more loopholes, and easy connectivity offers countless temptations for shortcuts around real learning. But kids want to do the right thing, and it's up to us as parents to help mentor them so that they make the right choices.

With many answers a simple Google search away, we need to offer kids some guidance on what constitutes original work. Some teachers are watching for such shortcuts and others are not, so as parents we have to help keep our kids on the up and up in this challenging arena. Kids recognize the attraction of easy answers, too. When I interviewed a group of seventh graders at a 1:1 middle school, they expressed worry that they would be tempted to cheat when using an iPad for homework.

Some kids absolutely know that they are cheating. In the same interview, one seventh grader described an app called Photomath that allowed him to hold his tablet up to a math worksheet and have the app scan the problems and immediately supply the answers. He understood that it wasn't okay to do his work this way, but thought that it might be okay to check answers using an app. One girl responded, "I know I won't learn the math if I use the app that way, but sometimes if I already get the concept, I don't think it would be so bad."

If you are unsure about an app your child is using for homework help, ask the teacher or have your child show you how it works. Many apps of this nature get classified as "educational," so that classification alone is not very helpful. On the other hand, apps like EasyBib, which formats bibliographic entries into whatever style you need, certainly would have made college and graduate school easier for me!

Crediting the Work of Others

Many kids do get some education about appropriate use of sources and how to cite sources, but with so much information at our fingertips, kids may ask, "Why should I write this myself?" I've had college students who thought it would be okay to take other people's published descriptions of films they watched in my courses and use them (uncredited!) in their papers. They felt that because their arguments were original and Siskel and Ebert had summarized the film well, they didn't need to bother writing original words to describe the film.

It's hard for kids to understand that, just because something is freely available on the web, it's not free to use. Today's kids have grown up in a remix culture, and they expect to be able to use whatever digital content is out there for their own purposes. While some educational uses of copyrighted material may be permitted, the rules of fair use are not clearly defined. Copyright violation can have serious consequences, so it's a good idea to instill in your kids a respect for the intellectual property of others.

A cute YouTube mash-up created by your child may seem innocent enough, but you wouldn't be happy to get a takedown notice from a corporate lawyer—or worse, a summons. We don't ever want to squelch our children's creative spirit, but it's worth teaching them the ground rules so that their endeavors are not only fun but safe, too.

Many schools, especially school librarians, are doing a great job teaching kids about credit and intellectual property, but this is not always the case. Or your child may compartmentalize the information in a way that means he doesn't consider what he learned in the library about writing a report applicable to that fun mash-up he is making. Any time you can talk about examples from your own work, you can help your children. As kids get older, the concept of fair use and even the ideas promoted at QuestionCopyright.org are worth engaging. But you need to know the rules before you can question them.

Collaborative Assignments

Working together and collaborating on homework is made easier by technology. Constant connection between classmates can enhance the learning experience, as ideas can flow back and forth in real time. The downside is that it is also easy for kids (especially those in middle and high school) to take pictures of tests and share them.

Many assignments today are collaborative. Just as you may have groaned in some circumstances about group work, your child may feel similarly. Collaboration can be tough! He may feel that not all members of the group pull their own weight. In any group, this is a real possibility. Wherever possible, see if the teacher offers a method for collaboration rather than expecting students to come up with a fair way to split the work on their own.

If the teacher is not forthcoming with collaboration plans, you can talk with your child, for example, about the virtues of simultaneous collaboration versus A/B collaboration (where you work on something, your partner edits and adds to it, and then it comes back to you for another edit). The larger the group, the harder it will be to collaborate simultaneously, unless specific roles are assigned.

Getting Practical

Here are some good questions to ask your kids to open a discussion about academic dishonesty:

- What is the difference between collaboration and cheating?
- Has anyone ever taken credit for your idea? How did you feel? What did you do?
- How do you know the difference between your own idea and someone else's idea?
- When is it okay to e-mail another student for help with your homework?
- What do you do if a classmate is constantly asking for your help? When is it okay to say no? How do you know when you should tell a parent or teacher?

When Schools Can't or Won't Enforce the Rules

Schools often have technology policies that are outdated or that they don't follow. The rapid pace of technology change and the complexities of updating policies can put schools in a bind. A few short years ago, elementary schools and even many middle schools didn't need policies for personal devices. Now they do!

I recently worked with a middle school where the stated rule was "No personal devices," but children had phones everywhere. The school clearly needed a better policy that acknowledged the realities of its students and worked with them proactively. Parents want to rely on schools to enforce rules, even though we sometimes would like exceptions for our own kids. The reality is that many schools don't enforce their own rules, and affluent suburban and independent schools are the least likely to use strong measures such as requiring all students to turn in their phones. While some parents with kids at these schools might wish for such enforcement, many others would object vociferously.

What can you do? Work with other parents in your community to demand that school policies are enforced, but be realistic. You have to recognize that, if devices are present at school, kids will not be completely cut off from them. But you can also support your child's obedience to the rules by not texting or phoning him at school during the school day. Also, if the school has multiple periods for recess, many adults agree that at least one should encourage physical activity. Parents can let schools know that this is a priority.

Many schools are making recess or lunch unplugged zones, and some are promoting phone-free Fridays. I like to see that schools are recognizing the issue and making an effort to help. But keep in mind that transitional times like recess or dismissal can be what

I call "zones of chaos," and it may be incredibly hard to enforce the rules during these times. Simply understanding that challenge can be helpful—at some elementary schools, parents can volunteer to monitor recess or lunch. Doing this even once will give you a sense of the way devices fit into these less structured times in the school day. If you find that technology is being used negative ways, a gaming or coding club could an excellent alternative to minimally supervised device access during recess or after school.

But What Am I Supposed to Do?

I hope that this section has shed new light on how you can best be involved in your child's education. Involvement is not just about taking an interest and enforcing the rules, it's about what you contribute and how you participate. You are not only modeling good digital citizenship for your kids, but for the entire community that is invested in your child's education.

Some big picture tips for navigating parenting a connected student:

- What steps can you take to help a teacher who is not so tech savvy?
- Before you (or your child) e-mail the teacher, do you model that you first try to resolve your question in another way?
- What strategies do you use to help with issues of distraction?
- Do you know how to log into the school's learning management system to check on your child's progress? Do you feel like this option is helpful or stressful?
- What do you do if you feel that your child is taking too long to finish his homework?

- A great book for diving further into a parent's perspective on the twenty-first century school experience is *Smart Parents: Parenting for Powerful Learning*, written by the learning specialists at GettingSmart.com.

- What guidance can you give to kids who work on collaborative assignments?

- Do you have a sense of how long your child's homework should take—and which parts require her to be online?

- How do you handle situations where schools don't enforce the technology rules they set?

CHAPTER 9

Growing Up in Public

Whether we like it or not, our kids have a digital reputation, also referred to as a *digital footprint*. Thus, we want to cement in their minds an understanding that what they create is associated with them. We don't want there to be a huge fear factor attached to this idea—we simply need to encourage kids who participate in social spaces to produce positive content, always. It's not that they can't be critical or disagree with something, but their tone should be constructive and sensitive to the feelings of others.

School is a great place to learn that what you publish or share with an audience is part of what people know about you. Having kids put their work out there (when they are ready)—and having people associate them with excellent and positive work—is a great way to make a clear connection between positive content and digital footprint.

Start with Awareness

Parents feel a lot of fear about social media and its effect on kids, but social media is not bad, in and of itself. It just turns up the dial on whatever is already happening with your child socially. Having a social media account will not transform your child's personality. But there are some inherent dangers, which is why it's good to be aware of what your kid is doing.

If your child knows you are—or might be—checking up on her, she may be encouraged to curb her own behavior. Research shows that more people wash their hands after using the bathroom when someone else is around. We all sit up a little straighter when another person is in the room. Knowing that supervision is a possibility can help your child make good choices. But even if you don't intend to supervise closely, you should remind kids that they might lose their phone or that someone else might be looking at it.

Social media on its own is not a threat to our kids—it is a question of how they use such platforms. Our connected world offers our children incredible opportunities. Teens have a variety of tools they can use to post their experiences and opinions, but sometimes they lack the sensibility to know what they should—or shouldn't—be posting.

Images As Digital Currency

As I discussed in chapter 2, photos are a big part of your kid's social world. It has never been easier to take, and share, photos. Some kids seem to see that as a personal challenge, and fill up the Internet with selfies and tagged friend pics.

We can bemoan our kids' fascination with photos or make light of it, but the fact is that digital images are a form of communication—and a really important one for today's young people. You can't just shut it off or forbid it, or you are ignoring a crucial skillset. Kids need to learn to interpret and communicate with images.

Photo Apps du Jour

At the time of writing, the predominant apps kids use to share photos are Instagram, Snapchat, and, to a lesser extent, Facebook. With WhatsApp, Kik, and other texing apps, they can also share photos and videos. With more than 1.5 billion people on Facebook, most of today's parents have at least some experience with this platform—some parents check in occasionally, while other parents are highly active users. So you may have some personal experience with photo sharing to draw on.

As I write, Instagram functions a little differently than Facebook. While you can annotate shared images on Facebook, Instagram is more about the photo itself. You can get creative with your photo, applying filters to change the image itself, but annotations are generally limited. This means that you really need to know someone to understand the context of the image. Snapchat speaks to a desire for ephemerality. The image disappears soon after the recipient opens it. Even a Snapchat story—a narrative conglomeration of "snaps"—has a twenty-four-hour life span.

Fifteen-year-old Ruby Karp writes that extensive social media use "captures the very real insecurities of teenagers. We don't want to seem like losers; therefore, we need to prove to people that we are still active in our 'social scene.' Instead of enjoying what we are doing, all we do is take pictures of what we are doing to make other teens feel bad they aren't with us."[1]

Since the story tends to feature socializing and is typically shared in real time, it can easily foster a user's insecurities. Am I at the best party? Is something better happening somewhere else? While teens like Karp seem to intellectually understand that their FOMO is often baseless—and that the other party may be just as boring as the one you are at—it doesn't make her (or her friends) put down their phones to be more present with the moment.[2]

By the time you hold this book in your hands, another app may have gained favor with your kids and their friends. We don't need to get caught up with the ins and outs of every app; instead, I want you to understand the desirability, culture, and potential pitfalls of the ones your kids actively use. The good news is, they can tell you about these!

Kids appreciate that they can speak in code by sharing photos that have contexts understood only by certain recipients. This is likely one of the reasons that Instagram has become so popular with teens and tweens (while Facebook has fallen out of favor with this age group). The same goes for Snapchat. Here's a good example. A picture of a teen wearing a sweatshirt with a college name on it would mean little to a stranger, but the kid's friends might know it means that she was accepted to that college today. The message is instantaneous, it's effective, and it's coded. It is a kind of self-expression and literacy we often don't appreciate.

How to Talk to Your Tween About Sexy Pictures

How do we address the topic of sexy pics exchanged by teens and younger kids? Parents and educators alike cringe when this topic comes up. Kids are becoming sexual in the tween years, but they are also interested in being provocative and doing what is forbidden. Many images that *don't* fall into the category of "sexting" still concern adults. It can be hard to articulate to your sixth-grade daughter why a photograph with her friends attempting pouty lips or flipping their hair feels inappropriate.

In *Sexy Baby,* a documentary about girls' and women's sexual representation in the digital age, a pivotal scene features twelve-year-old Winnifred and a friend doing a photo shoot around the subject's modern Brooklyn apartment.[3] The girls drape themselves over furniture, let their clothes hang off their shoulders, and imply "sexiness" in a very twelve-year-old way. Winnifred's father reminds them not to post any of the pictures, but they can't resist the temptation to share the images with peers. The next scene we see is an angry confrontation between the girl, Winnifred, and her mother. Winnifred is crying. She is more upset that her mother called the photos slutty than she is to be in trouble. Girls this age are in a bind. Later in the film Winnifred says you have to appear as if you are "down to f__" but then you see her scrolling through her gymnastics photos and are reminded that she is, in many ways, still just a young girl.

The mother's reaction came from an emotional place, and she probably regretted her choice of words. We don't want to use negative labels when we talk with our kids about photos; instead, you could say, "I know it there is pressure to try to look sexy, but you are too young to post pictures that invite people to look at you that way. You are beautiful, but I don't want you to feel you need people to say that to you all the time." Boys are less likely to feel overwhelming pressure to look "hot" in sixth or seventh grade, but they may be pressured to look at sexy images or pornography.

According to adolescent communication researcher Susannah Stern, it is worth having a discussion rather than lecturing our kids about sexting. Help kids understand that pictures can be taken out of context, and ask them to think about how their future self might feel about an image.[4]

When I speak to students, I talk with them about consent. They should never feel pressured to send a picture of themselves or do it to try to win favor or attention. And if kids receive an inappropriate picture, they need to know they should not share it further. Even if the photo is being passed all over school, they should recognize this as nonconsensual sharing and not participate. But Stern points out that curiosity and interest in sex and sexual feelings are normal parts of adolescent development. In other words, creating and sharing a picture doesn't mean there is something terribly wrong with your child, but we don't live in a society where this is a safe way to explore sexuality.

Stern also points out the vastly different social consequences for boys and girls who take and share sexy pictures, as well as the fact that we live in a society where we sexualize girls to a high degree. When girls' and women's bodies are objectified in such pervasive ways in media and popular culture, it is not outlandish for girls to get the idea that sending sexy pictures is a good way to flirt or relate to boys. And it is not entirely out of keeping with social norms that boys might think it is okay to keep images of a particular girl or even many girls (however much we might want to change those norms). That doesn't mean you have to accept this behavior, but if your son or one of his friends thinks it is perfectly okay to have pictures of girls on his phone, he is probably getting that idea from others around him.

If you find out that your child has shared an image of him- or herself or has received an inappropriate image of a peer, try to learn more about the context before you panic. If the context was coercive, that is a problem of significant magnitude. If the context was consensual at one time, but is no longer (i.e., an ex-partner circulates an image), that is also a concerning scenario. If the images were consensually exchanged and your child does not feel harmed or embarrassed, then that is the best-case scenario in what is admittedly challenging terrain.

When I speak to kids, I emphasize that if they receive a

questionable image—unless it was sent directly to them by the subject—they should understand that it was *not* intended for them. Circulating images without consent is an ethical violation. The legal ramifications are significant, too, but I especially focus on our collective obligation not to amplify harm by circulating an image that has gotten out of the subject's control. If your child or one of his friends is in a situation where a photo is "out there," you may wish to consult other resources, such as a booklet called "So You Got Naked Online." Published in the U.K. and available for download, it has great advice for young people who find themselves in this situation (swgfl.org.uk/products-services/esafety /resources/So-You-Got-Naked-Online).

Understanding Who Your Audience Is

danah boyd, a researcher at Microsoft, has done groundbreaking work that helps us understand some of young people's perceptions about growing up in networked social spaces. In her book *It's Complicated,* boyd cites an example of a young person who posted on Facebook and got a response from someone unexpected. While the post was intended for his friends, the guy's family (and other connections) could see it too. When his older sister, who's away at college, responds to his post, "aw baby bro," it feels invasive to him. He thinks, "No, I wasn't talking to you," despite the fact that the post was shared with all his connections.[5]

boyd points out that adults use social media differently than young people. Social media is a "second space" for young people, where they can hang out virtually even when they are not with their friends physically. Young teens/tweens' identities are in flux, so they may be especially attracted to the ephemeral nature of social apps such as Snapchat. Platforms such as Facebook can still be attractive, but the long memory of a Facebook wall post may be one of the reasons that Facebook is losing popularity among thirteen- to seventeen-year-olds. boyd notes, "One of the reasons all of this visual stuff (like Snapchat) is coming down the line right now is because people don't want to be searchable all the time."[6] So the more ephemeral apps, where photos are supposed to disappear (Snapchat) or get buried in a busy feed (Instagram), might be more attractive to young people than Facebook, with its photo album feel and easy-to-search archives. Indeed, I enjoy my "year in review" on Facebook in part because I am an adult. I've got the same friends and hairstyle and tastes that I did a year ago, so the year in review is a pleasant experience, not a reminder of an identity I'd like to distance myself from.

One of the challenges for any of us, but especially for kids new to social media, is that we may forget who sees our posts. We may have in mind only small segments of our potential audience and may share things intended for a few friends, forgetting that others might see what we share. Interestingly, kids who do this sometimes feel angry or violated when those people (including parents) comment or react, even though they shared the image or text publicly. We can remind our children that other people may share what we post. Even when privacy settings are turned on, kids should remember that they don't have carte blanche to say whatever comes to mind. Everything can be shared and reshared.

Some kids will participate on apps such as Omegle to "talk to strangers," but for the most part, they are interested in interacting with other kids they already know or who are connected to people they know in person. Social media feels like a peer space to them. Elliot and Jonathan, my Minecraft-playing informants, told me that playing with people they don't know is "okay, but it can be weird, or they might start speaking another language." Mostly, when they go onto public servers, they seek out the kids they know personally. Other kids have told me about people speaking to them or messaging them from games and that it can feel "creepy."

Another challenge of social media and contact lists is friend curation—knowing who to follow, friend, share your phone number with, etc. Adrian, an eighth grader, told me that "if you know someone, or if you've, like, heard of them, usually you will let them follow. And you follow back, because it is weird not to." We can remind our kids that they don't need to follow everyone they have "heard of" and also encourage them to clean up their contacts periodically, removing people they can't remember, for instance. If your child shared his phone number with the entire town during group texting in sixth grade, a new phone number for high school might be a helpful restart.

As I mentioned, kids may be thinking about a certain audience and not others when they post. It is good to remember the whole crowd, and to know that other people may share what we post. We adults may have learned not to write e-mails we wouldn't want forwarded, but many of us have done it, despite knowing better.

Questions to ask your kids:

- When is it a good idea not to let someone follow you, or even to block them?
- Do you feel like it is rude not to connect on social media if someone initiates a connection with you?
- Can you think of a time when you posted something and someone you were not expecting commented on it? How did that make you feel?

Quantifying Popularity

How do you deal with the quantifiable nature of likes and followers? I confess that I've had my moments: after my TEDx Talk was shared on Upworthy, the number of views climbed daily by the hundreds for a few weeks. I found myself checking several times a day that week and admit that the upticks were somewhat intoxicating.

As kids build networks, help them identify who they should accept as a connection or follower. They shouldn't follow someone just to track that person's moves. Often, kids want to follow kids who are well known at school, the popular kids. But is it really fun to know what those kids are doing if you aren't really friends with them, if their activities don't include you? Even adults sometimes quantify their numbers on social media, although adults often look askance at those whose connections seem dominated by weak ties. The numbers and types of connections deemed appropriate are somewhat medium specific/app specific. Having a large following may make sense on Twitter or Instagram, for example, but Facebook has tended toward a more mutual set of relations, except for celebrity or business pages.

After I conducted focus groups with seventh-grade girls, it became apparent that "too many" followers or social media connections was defined as about 25 percent more than the individual definer had. So if one girl has three hundred Instagram followers, then "too many" is more than five hundred.

In contrast to kids, many of whom are trapped with a peer group in school year after year, most adults see their relationships outside the rubric of "popular/unpopular." The work of sustaining friendships while juggling career and family necessarily winnows many of our adult social circles to predominantly friends we actually like—possibly old friends we made in college or when we had more time in our twenties, or friends cultivated in the trenches of work and parenthood.

Kids Who Abstain from Social Media

Some kids share on the Internet without being part of social media. I know a very thoughtful and artistic young girl, Annie, who goes to a large public school and eats lunch with her best friend every day. Annie doesn't have a wide circle of friends, and is a fairly introverted and reserved kid. This girl is a talented artist and makes interesting work out of recycled materials. Her mother helped her register with her city's young artists' website. There, she can show her work, as well as on other sites such as Etsy. She can communicate with other young artists, share her work, and receive feedback.

There are many ways to be social both online *and* offline without social media. This young girl's parents would not want her, at the age of eleven, to be on Instagram. Their daughter agrees—she has no desire to take lots of pictures of herself and her friends and share them publicly, which is a big part of many social media platforms.

Some kids also abstain from social media after a bad experience or because they just don't like it. This can be a restorative and helpful break. If your child eschews social media, I wouldn't worry, especially if it seems in keeping with her personality. Closing accounts and getting off all social media suddenly could be a red flag that something is seriously wrong, however—that is definitely something to keep an eye on.

Social Identity in a New World

As a result of growing up with social media, the kids in my focus groups and workshops have a finely tuned sense of their public presence to their peers. For the most part, they are much more focused on what their profiles mean in the micro world of their own school or social scene than in the macro world strangers inhabit.

As parents, we need to understand enough about the culture of our kids' social media world that we can support and mentor them. That doesn't mean we need to be part of that culture or (heaven forbid) use their slang. But we should realize that, from the outside, the way kids game together, group text, or hang out on social media may seem like chaos or anarchy; from the inside, however, kids are often following rules that are not explicitly stated—but you know it if you blow it! Finding out how your kids feel about these rules and their role in these micro cultures is more important than trying to keep track of the minutiae of the rules or the apps themselves.

Most of the time, our kids' vigilance about impression management is not geared toward future employers but to people at their school or in the world where they are trying to find their place. Kids can post and predict how quickly the "likes" and comments will come in. If they are incorrect, they may be embarrassed and will sometimes remove a post. The three New York City ninth-grade girls I quoted in chapter 7 posted a picture from the studio during their interview with Ira Glass, then discussed it:

Ira Glass: So what's your prediction on what's going to happen?
Ella: Usually there's at least—usually there's two likes in a minute. But I don't know, because people might not be up yet.
Ira Glass: It was 11:00 in the morning on a day with no school,

not prime time for posting photos at all. Nighttime is usually when you get the most likes and comments. But, you know, 11:00 a.m. A minute passes. No response on the photo they took in the studio. And then?

Ella: Oh, wait, three likes.

Julia: Oh, three likes.

Jane: From Ro—

Ella: From three people. No one's commented yet. One of these is my best friend. Okay, another person liked it. Two people.

Jane: Two people. Okay, we're getting a lot of likes now.

Ella: Three. Another person.

Jane: How many likes do we have now?

Ella: Six, I think.

Jane: Okay, we have one, two, three, four, five, six likes in a minute. That's actually good, Ella.

The need for a response to what we share, and the predictability of that response, is part of growing up in public. But we don't want our kids to be dependent on likes, so how do we help them? It is important to understand that kids this age have somewhat rigid social rules that are implied. The rules are: we can't tell you what they are, but we'll ice you out if you break them.

Giving kids a chance to talk about "the rules" and even explaining to less savvy kids that there tend to be some unspoken rules about peer interactions is a helpful step. If your kid steps on a landmine by violating some rule she didn't know, be supportive. Your aim is not to get your child to become a compulsive rule follower but to empower her to make choices with at least some understanding of the peer landscape. For more on surviving middle school social cliques and other issues, you might check out Rachel Simmons's *Odd Girl Out*, Michelle Icard's *Middle School Makeover*, and Rosalind Wiseman's *Masterminds and Wingmen* and *Queen Bees and Wannabes.*

Breaking the Social Code

In one of my focus groups with seventh-grade girls in an affluent suburb, all the girls had iPhones and were avid Instagram users (except for one, who had an iPhone but chose not to use Instagram). The others were all very attuned to their images, and they had a definite set of "rules" about pictures.

Somewhat aware of their privileged socioeconomic status, they talked about how it would *not* be okay to share vacation pictures of a fancy hotel, the pool, etc. They used an example of a particular classmate, Jocelyn, who had (unknowingly) violated this rule. The rule, like many unspoken social rules, became clear and vivid to these girls by its violation.

Jocelyn had returned from a lavish vacation at a foreign resort and had shown pictures of the vacation as part of a school project. This galled the other girls, as they felt the "educational" value of the trip was nil. In fact, they identified this behavior as an immature form of bragging. They were able to give many examples of other kids—presumably also very privileged—who had gone on even "better trips" or lived in "amazing houses," but who "knew better" than to post about it.

Peer Judgment of Sexuality

Jocelyn, who displayed her vacation photos, was also targeted for posting a bikini photo from the same trip, despite having "nothing to put in a bikini." After some probing, I learned that there are also social rules for when it might be okay to share a picture with one friend and not another, when it would be appropriate to post bathing suit pictures, and other special cases. The girls had heard from adults about not sharing pictures that were too revealing or "too sexy." But they clearly also had their own standards by which they judged peers.

Of all the judgments they may be subject to, peer judgments are the ones kids most fear. Unfortunately, based on my conversations with both kids and adults, sexist double standards are commonplace in both urban and suburban communities. Unwritten social rules about bikini posts show that girls walk a thin line: being attractive is good, but being "too sexy" or "trying too hard" is bad. Being too sexy can also quickly lead to "slut shaming," and what kids still call a "bad reputation," just like we did when we were kids.

Because I was an impartial outsider (and because I ask a lot of questions), the girls explained "the bikini rule" more explicitly and revealed more about the rules than they might have otherwise. Their bikini rule was, "You can post a bikini or bathing suit picture if you are with your siblings or your family." All the girls agreed on some form of this rule. In other words, don't try too hard to be sexy, and you will be okay. These girls want to be seen as pretty and sexy in some ways, but they are also young enough to want to be seen as innocent. The culture tells them to be a little sexy but not to be seen as wanting to be sexy. This is a tough balance to manage at any age, but it's impossible in seventh grade. Indeed, this "immature girl" with "nothing to put in her bikini" broke one side of the social rules. Let's look at the other side now.

The girls identified another peer who broke the social code, but in a different way. This particular seventh grader was seen as too sexual. Some of the girls even said that their moms did not want them to hang out with the "too sexy" girl. The problem was exposed via text message, unfortunately. "My mom doesn't want me to hang out with M____" was shared in a group text where (oops) this girl was actually present. These missteps only fan the flames and make the problem worse.

Boys also face judgment about sexuality that can be challenging in the world of social media. They can become self-conscious about body image and may also face strong pressure to look at porn or sexual images as part of "boy culture." It is important to let boys know that they don't have to do this and that these images decontextualize sex. They should understand that real girls and women will not respond in the same ways that actors do in the scenarios they see depicted.

An important part of parenting both boys and girls is helping them cultivate a strong, positive self-image that includes sexuality but does not objectify themselves or others. Youth groups, scouting groups, and volunteer work opportunities in the community can make welcome partners for parents in this challenging endeavor.

What Can We Do to Help?

Without being too alarmist, I do think that parents should pay attention to the amount of time and energy their kids are putting into cultivating their online image. The particular rules described above are salient for the seventh-grade girls in that community—but a unique set of social rules exists in every community.

Recognizing the existence of social norms is good start—and it can be a good way to get kids to talk about their own particular culture. Identifying the social norms will help you and your child

understand how social media, group texting, and other digital interactions are negotiated in your child's world. The emergence of these
(usually) unspoken rules shows how closely kids are watching and
policing what others share, and how much they pay attention to
what they share themselves. All good information in the hands of
mentors like you.

Encouraging kids to resist strong negative judgments about other
kids, and helping them deal with the stresses of knowing that what
they share can be judged harshly, is important. Even though your
kids are forming their own society, they don't need to feel they are
navigating the sometimes confusing or random rules on their own.

Good questions to ask your kids:

- If you were making a social media (or name the specific app
  they love) handbook for exchange students from another cul-
  ture, what would you tell them so they could avoid a faux pas?
- Is that "rule" the same for boys and girls? Why or why not?
- What are some "rules" that you can change?
- Does social media ever stress you out?
- How can you give yourself a break?
- Do kids ever post things just to be liked?
- Should people take something down if few people respond?

Visual Self-Representation

When I show pictures of other kids to the kids in my workshops,
they are filled with judgments. They will often say, "He's a slob,"
"She's trying too hard," "Stupid smile," or famously, at one school in
Indianapolis, the kids said "Carmel," the name of an affluent sub-
urb. The photo was actually of a kid from an affluent suburb of
Minneapolis. So the students were incorrect, but also correct, in a

way. These kids were applying context and injecting assumptions based on their own sense of social geography. The conversations reveal how finely tuned kids' senses can become about contextual clues from faces, clothing, and location. In this example, the subject was standing in a green area in front of a driveway or cul-de-sac—so the guess about suburbia made sense. But what about the kids who said one girl was "full of herself"? A screenwise approach isn't about eliminating judgment completely. Instead, we should help kids recognize and examine their initial judgments, and help them understand that people who don't know them are prone to making snap judgments based on their photographs.

We can model appropriate ways to judge other people. Try this exercise with your kids: show them pictures of other kids and ask for their judgment. When they don't know the person or context, they can be judgmental and mean. But our kids do understand context. We can model being nonjudgmental. Point out to them that we don't really know anything about the person except for external cues. Introduce other possibilities and other scenarios.

When I ask groups of eighth graders if they have ever seen a picture of a person before meeting her, almost all of them raise their hands. Then I ask them if they have ever been surprised by what the person is like in real life after the impression they formed from the photo, and many raise their hands again.

Your Child's Digital Footprint

I love the term "digital footprint." To me, it signifies that we are taking steps forward—progress is good. But with every step, we are leaving something behind as well. Sometimes that footprint might fade quickly, like walking in the sand on a windy day. Sometimes it might be more lasting, like stepping in wet cement. The context matters.

Footprints are an apt metaphor because, whether we are aware of it or not, we leave behind traces of ourselves in the digital world. Every time we post a picture on Facebook, send an e-mail, or even make a call with a cell phone, we create data. With enough data, a picture forms—where we were, what we were doing, and who we were with.

Framed against yesterday's world, this seems kind of creepy. You may even feel tempted to go "off the grid." But we trade modern conveniences for this seemingly minor inconvenience every day. So let's get realistic and dive into ways to manage our digital footprints—and, more importantly, how to help our kids understand data collection so they can make better decisions.

Getting Rid of the Gotcha

Parents and educators alike can get very worried about kids' digital footprints. While some caution is warranted, there's a lot of mythology around this too. How many times have you heard negative stories of social media gone wrong, featuring reputations that have been damaged permanently and irreparably?

I really hate the poisonous "gotcha" genre of takedown via social media. It is mean spirited to laugh when an irresponsible tweet gets someone fired from a job. The kid who hated her summer job uniform and tweeted about it made an error in judgment. Yes, it was her fault—she sent the tweet. But should we relish the thought of a kid losing a summer job she might have really needed? Do hundreds of people need to pile on? Losing her job was already a steep price to pay![7]

Kids are vulnerable to these missteps, as they are still figuring out the line between what is funny and what is not. We as parents (and teachers) have to be careful that we don't commit the same mistakes. Pointing out a child's misstep shouldn't feel like a "gotcha!" moment. Kids are exploring and learning how to interact, healthy activities that need to be nourished. The reality is that we need to help them, but even more importantly, we need to teach them how to repair the damage when they have made an error. How can they ask for forgiveness? How can they get it right the next time?

When I was sixteen, I had a friend who made a lot of questionable Hitler jokes. In yesterday's schoolyard or dormitory, these jokes—while offensive—were not permanently recorded. Today, he has a very powerful job in the motion picture industry. He still has an offbeat sense of humor, but he's smart enough as an adult not to tweet a Hitler joke.

Fast-forward to today's kids. An offensive joke posted on Instagram, Twitter, or Snapchat (yes, even Snapchat!) might stick around for years. For all intents and purposes, the post is permanent. Social media, and digital communication in general, feels ephemeral, but we shouldn't be fooled. Good digital citizenship means that we conduct ourselves online just as we would offline.

Speaking of which, when a friend or classmate posts something genuinely offensive—or even hits the wrong note—we need to teach kids how to gracefully say, "I know you thought that was funny, but it wasn't."

Try the following conversation starters with your kids:

- Have you ever seen someone try to be funny in a group text but hurt people's feelings instead?
- Do you think people ever say "JK" or "it was just a joke" when they are being mean?

Training Wheels for Sharing

In my experience helping parents manage their kids' digital footprint, I find that parents often worry about the wrong things, and tend to focus too much on the downsides. Your child will get hired after college, even if there are some spelling errors in the Tumblr blog she kept as a twelve-year-old.

Adults should encourage kids to put their best work and best self out there, doing things they can be proud of. This is more helpful than attempting to "hide" wrongdoings and/or "scrubbing" their reputations. This can be a great way for kids to learn about creativity. A class blog in a school sharing community is a fantastic place for your child to learn about the potential upsides of getting "known" for his work.

Teachers or coaches who know and understand your child are in a good position to help if there is any serious story that needs further explanation when your child is applying to college. Mistakes can be understood in context and addressed, if need be.

Proper Profile Maintenance

I suggest doing a privacy audit of every single social media account you and your children have at least two to three times per year to see what a public search can pick up. Is your child sharing videos and pictures? Doing a search on one or two top search engines is a good idea. If you find something you don't like, there are numerous approaches you can take. You can contact the person who has posted the image or text and ask him to take it down. For example, social media posts shared with minimal privacy settings sometimes come up in Internet searches. If a post is in your child's own social media stream, he may be able to remove it. While it is not completely "erased" from the Internet's archives, taking down the post will make it less likely to appear in search results over time.

Authentic Audiences and Civil Interactions

One of the simplest ways to mentor kids on civil interactions is through the blog's comments section. We want kids to do things like set their own blog comments policy; they often suggest guidelines such as, "You need to read my whole post before you comment." How many rancorous comments sections have you witnessed where adults have failed to follow this sensible policy?

Alternatively, comments might be set up so they need to be approved—and parents can filter them. This can be a lot of work, though! It may seem easier to just keep your kid off digital media completely. If you are in a position where you can't mentor due to time or other constraints, that may be a good way to go.

Further, the tone of comments is something to which kids are sensitive. Conflict of any sort is difficult to manage, even for adults. When an interaction is online, there's a layer of complexity added, in that it's harder to have empathy for someone you've never met in person and with the only context being one comment on a blog!

As an exercise, ask your kids:

- Should you respond to a blog post you don't agree with? When should you not respond?
- How can you appropriately and respectfully disagree with something you've read?
- When you disagree, do you use evidence and a proper argument to refute the argument?
- What should you do (or not do) when someone posts a mean comment about someone else?

Talking about these issues with kids up front situates the issues in their minds. They will still need to learn by doing, but the discussion will provide some guidance as they learn. Having kids set their own policies can help them understand balance: if they govern the comments section too much, there will be less engagement, but if they leave it totally unbounded, someone could get hurt or the conversation may be less productive and meaningful. This is a great life lesson.

Leaving a Data Trail

Social media is not free. While we don't pay to use Facebook or Google or other social platforms, that doesn't mean that they are without a cost. You "pay" for each of these services with data. Whether you read it or not, you clicked "I agree" to each platform's terms of service (TOS) or end user license agreement (EULA). These documents are purposely abstruse, but the gist is essentially this: in exchange for using our platform free of charge, you agree that we can make use of the data generated by your interactions.

Sounds scary, right? While I don't believe that these companies have nefarious aims, they are certainly more commercial than benevolent. Their business models are built upon the trust of their users, so it would not likely be in their best interest to erode that trust. But it's good to be aware of how they are using your data so that you can "tune" what you share to your comfort level and teach your kids to do the same.

You are leaving a data trail with everything you do. Most of these companies are not looking at (nor do they care about) your individual posts and comments—they use "bots" to scrape your content for keywords. Is this harmful? Some would argue that it's not. Whatever your feelings about it, the knowledge of how your data is used should affect the way you employ social media. With every interaction you are producing data, and this data is painting a picture of you. The only way to control it is to adjust the data you feed into the system.

Geo-Tagging

One of the first things to look at—yet not always the most obvious—is broadcasting your location. Sit down with your kids and look at settings with them as they set up or update accounts. The geo-tagging setting may default to sharing your location, without you even thinking about it.

Talk with your child and see how she feels about geo-tagging. Together, come up with some reasons that it might not be great to let everyone know where you are with each shared post. Aside from some obvious safety issues, has she considered the possibility that her check-ins might cause hurt feelings among her friends? Sometimes sharing not in real time is a strategy kids use to defuse the intensity of being excluded from things. But with geo-tagging, knowing where you were yesterday (or even an hour ago!) can lead to problems between friends.

Privacy and Oversharing

As I said earlier in this chapter, parents (and other adults) harbor a persistent belief that today's kids have no regard for privacy. Their evidence? A teenager's "rant" on Facebook, an inappropriate divulgence via Twitter, a photo that would have been better saved than shared.

I still remember walking home from seventh grade with a friend who told me she hated her parents. I had never dared to think something like that, let alone say it aloud. I rolled it around in my head. As I got to know her, I realized she had good reason to be deeply angry with her folks. But communicating her truth to me was both more private and more profound. Now consider the same message, this time conveyed via social media. "I hate my parents" could easily be taken as lighthearted or a joke—or it could be much more serious than that.

The fact is that these two social spaces are vastly different. The issue is not that kids don't have a sense of privacy, but instead that they lack an understanding of how to manage each of these terrains. Teaching kids how to manage these distinctions is tricky.

Say, for example, that you are angry with a friend. You need to vent. You call another friend of yours and do just that. You unload all the details. You feel better. Yes, there's a risk in this—the venting conversation might get back to the first friend. But imagine how different that would be if you instead vented about your friend on Tumblr, and she discovered the post three weeks later? The issue may actually have been resolved in person by that point, but social media will "remember." For all intents and purposes, it's a permanent record, even though it feels ephemeral. This is incredibly challenging for kids to understand. So what can you do?

- Set a social media policy for your family—what should and should not be shared. Talk about the guidelines directly.
- Walk through hypothetical situations, using real friends and family. That way, your kids will understand the policy in the context of real empathy and emotions.
- Have your kids look for and point out things that their peers are doing "wrong." This will get them to cast a critical eye on social interactions, using real examples, and will give you a window into their judgment.

Getting Screenwise Is a Process

While the issues I brought up in this chapter are not always fun to contemplate, I hope that you feel encouraged and not too overwhelmed. Many of the pitfalls that kids can run into via their devices and the Internet were present in our world, too. Connectivity just adds a layer of complexity to these issues. Sometimes it makes these dangers more apparent to adults, and sometimes it does amplify them. But let's not forget the opportunities our kids have to learn, create, and share their work in a connected world. When we mentor kids well, the opportunities can far outweigh the challenges.

CONCLUSION

Digital Citizenship for the Next Generation

Our kids' future success will depend on true digital fluency. Their ability to relate to other people and to succeed in their relationships is completely dependent on developing a strong digital skill set. This digital skill set:

- Is an immediate priority. If they don't start to develop it now, they won't succeed in today's—or tomorrow's—world.
- Is not operational or functional. It is not about how to keyboard or how to code. Anyone can learn those skills, with enough practice.
- Is about relationships. It's about the kinds of connections we can have with one another. It's about trust.

Nuances matter. Even if you feel overwhelmed, you can be a great mentor. But you have to learn in order to teach:

- Your ability to parent, lead, or teach is affected by your own relationship with technology.
- Your relationship with technology is a model for your kids. Learning about their world is a requirement.

- You have the capacity to relate well to other people. You have the capacity to teach these principles to others.
- You can't disconnect and say, "I just don't get this." Your kids are relying on you to be their guide in this new world.
- As parents and mentors, we need to understand and prepare for new milestones (first e-mail account, first phone, etc.), and prepare our kids for them.

Conditions are favorable:

- Good news. Kids actually want mentorship. They want and need advice on relating in the digital age.
- Good news. Digital literacy involves a skill set—*it can be learned.*
- Good news. Kids may be tech savvy, but you have wisdom. You hold the most powerful piece of the puzzle.

Taking this book as a jumping-off point for conversations with your child, you will find that you:

- Get closer to your kids and reduce stress in their lives.
- Increase trust between you and your kids.

Your mentorship will help your kids:

- Elevate their social skills and feel more in control.
- Get better at managing repair.
- Feel like you are listening to their concerns.

Armed with a little knowledge and after some regular practice, you can make a positive difference in the lives of your children.

I hope I've convinced you that you don't have to know everything about every app and device to mentor your children. But you do need to be in the conversation. If you're not part of their world, you can't influence their world. I also hope I've made the case that the kids are (mostly) doing great. Not *everything* is cause for concern.

Mentorship is the single most important commitment we can make to our kids. It doesn't matter whether we are parents, teachers, school leaders, or administrators. If we interact with kids regularly, we are part of a community where mentorship is our responsibility.

Mentoring over Monitoring

Mentors start from a place of empathy as a path to trust and open communication.

Mentors see that kids are very creative and insightful, but that they still need models and they still need help navigating this world.

Mentors recognize that tech savvy is not the same as wisdom. Our life experience is a critical factor in the equation.

Mentors believe in collaboration over control. Cocreating solutions with kids takes advantage of their creativity and builds trust at the same time.

Mentors recognize the need to observe kids in their habitat in order to get a better understanding of their lived experiences.

Mentors recognize that the realm of social interactions is more complex now, and that kids need help in order to build good personal relationships.

Mentors believe in the power of curiosity to activate young minds.

Mentors don't want to *catch* their kids doing the wrong thing; they want to *teach* their kids to do the right thing!

Mentors believe in creativity over consumption. Not all screen time is created equal.

Mentors understand that tech limits alone are no substitute for engagement. Monitoring degrades trust and engenders a false sense of control.

Mentors understand that part of growing up is about experimenting with identities, and that issues around digital footprints can constrain kids in the wrong way at the wrong time.

Mentors are ready to be accountable to kids, in turn. The good and bad habits we harbor with technology serve as a model for kids.

Mentors provide room for learning and self-discovery, making plans that don't come from our anxiety and desire for control.

Mentors lead their families, teams, and community in service of a positive digital world for the next generation.

Raising Digital Natives: It's Up to Us

We need to solve the problems that arise in the digital world together, or we run the risk of a new generation that doesn't take full advantage of the possibilities before us. Burying our heads in the sand or trying to limit our kids' screen time is not going to take us to the next level.

- We are optimists. We don't make assumptions about what kids do with technology. We give them a chance and we stick to the facts. We don't succumb to fear.

- We are tech positive. But though we believe that technology can be a positive force, we don't think that it is all-powerful.

- We believe in curiosity. Technology is a means to learn, to do other things. Kids' minds are alive. If used properly, technology unlocks kids' natural creativity.

- We get excited about kids and their creativity. We believe that we can learn from kids as much as they can learn from us.

- We recognize that misunderstandings happen all the time between adults and kids. We commit to getting better at identifying and addressing these gaps in understanding.

- We believe that kids are fascinating, and that we need to study them in their habitat to truly understand them. We want to be invited into their world.

Let's make a commitment today, to our kids and to one another. The way we interact and communicate will keep changing, but one thing remains the same: true digital citizenship is our responsibility, and the stakes are too high to leave it to chance. It's vital for our kids, good for our families, and necessary for our communities.

Let's stand up. Let's be mentors. It's up to us.

Acknowledgments

Leaving the familiar world of higher education to found Raising Digital Natives has been at once exhilarating, overwhelming and immensely rewarding. I am so grateful to the parents, educators, and young people who have opened up to me and shared their stories of the pleasures and challenges of growing up in these times.

I am grateful to Jill Friedlander and Erika Heilman for their insightful support and excitement about this book. Susan Lauzau's editorial vision kept the book from going off the rails, and Jill Schoenhaut's wisdom made the book whole. Thank you for your patience and wisdom in the editorial process! Thanks also to Alicia Simons, Ari Choquette, and Shevaun Betzler at Bibliomotion for their insights and vision for bringing *Screenwise* into the world; it is a privilege to be part of the Bibliomotion community of authors. Fellow author Vicki Hoefle has been a guiding light in thinking about how to be of service to parents.

Thanks also to Ron Lieber, Mary O'Donohue, Deborah Gilboa, Annie Fox, Deborah Siegel, and Carrie Goldman, who shared sage advice about the book journey. The Raising Digital Natives Facebook discussion group—made up of some very smart parents and educators—has offered brilliance in an ongoing fashion. Jeanne Warsaw-Gazga, Michelle Linford, Shoshana Waskow, Maria Zabala, Jeanne Marie Olson, Ellen Zemel, Melissa Davis, and other members of that community have contributed much to my thinking on these topics. I am further grateful for Jennifer Forsberg, RoiAnn Philips, Debi Lewis, Peter Eckstein, Cassie Bell, and Amy Newman—and all the other smart, generous people who gave me feedback on this book. I could not have written this book without without content genius and big-picture thinker Michael Boezi. From the TEDx talk to *Screenwise*, Michael's questions are always the right ones, and I am grateful to have Michael on the team. Mandi Holmes keeps Raising Digital Natives running smoothly, and Alicia Senior-Saywell is going to save me from myself. Natasha Vorompiova masterminded amazing systems, and Christy Hruska helped me implement them. Karrie Kohlhaas offered brilliant strategy and coaching, and helped me see the need for this work in the world. Carolyn Ou tried to help me find work/ life balance. Jessie Shternshus is my role model, an amazing creative genius and and friend—so it is lucky she is also my cousin. Jill Salzman lights the way for so many great founders, and everyone should have her introduce their TEDx talk. I've learned so much and had so much fun collaborating with Karen Jacobson. Eileen Rochford and Jeanne Segal are both public relations superstars and insightful parents of teens.

The following friends helped keep me sane during a crazy year of writing and travel: Nadia Oehlson, Gilit Abraham, Michael Davis, Mary Abowd, Loren Lybarger, Sarah Levine, Sunny Schwartz, Moira Hinderer, Liz Duffrin, Joanie Friedman, Jon Stoper, Lisa and Dan Sniderman, Lori Baptista, Todd Krichmar, Naomi Schrag, Marv Hoffman, Rosellen Brown, Tamar and Elliot Frolichstein-Appel. Thanks to Sara Aye for being an amazing thought partner and friend and for coming up with the title for the book! My other fellow-founder friends like Stephanie Schwab, Ginger Malin, Kristen Hoffman Senior, and Shelley Prevost are an ongoing source of inspiration and support. Thanks also to my many friends with little kids, middle schoolers, and teenagers who shared their stories and inspiration.

Audiences at schools and conferences across the country gave valuable feedback on these ideas at various stages. Questions from audience members have shaped this book and are occasionally quoted (with different names). Thank you! Too many talented educators have influenced my thinking about mentoring kids in the digital age to include them all here, but I want to acknowledge the work of: Jill Maraldo, Jean Robbins, Dave Palzet, Steve Dembo, Carl Hooker, Chip Donohue, Amanda Armstrong, and Tamara Kaldor. Gratitude is also due to David Kleeman, Debra Hafner, Susannah Stern, Alex Pang, Deborah Roffman, and the other experts who spoke to me about their work as I drafted this book. Thanks to Ira Glass and the staff of *This American Life* for kind permission to quote from their thoughtful and inspiring show. Hundreds of young people have shared their insights with me about their perspective on growing up in a digital world. I hope this work does their perspectives justice, and I look forward to reading what they will write in the coming years.

My family is incredible, and I am grateful to you all for sharing my work, supporting this journey, and taking Harold on adventures while I was working and off on speaking engagements. Hilarious texts from my fabulous sister Sarah Heitner are welcome distractions. Ethan Heitner is always inspiring and supportive, and Antonia House is the best. I am most grateful to Seth and Glenn Goldman and their wonderful families for our fabulous modern family.

Howard and Lois Heitner and Lenore Weissmann are incredible grandparents and supportive parents as well.

My deepest thanks and love go to my husband, Dan Weissmann. Thank you for putting up with my travel and writing schedule, for your wise editorial counsel, and for supporting me in all things. You and Harold are the lights of my life.

Notes

Introduction

1. Marc Prensky, "Digital Natives, Digital Immigrants Part 1", *On the Horizon,* Vol. 5 No. 9, 1–6, (October 2001). http://www.marcprensky.com/writing/Prensky%20-%20Digital%20Natives,%20Digital%20Immigrants%20-%20Part1.pdf
2. Eszter Hargittai, "Digital Na(t)ives? Variation in Internet Skills and Uses Among Members of the "Net Generation"." *Sociological Inquiry* Vol. 80 Issue 1, 92–113. (February 2010). http://www.webuse.org/pdf/Hargittai-DigitalNativesSI2010.pdf
3. Alexandra Samuel, "Parents: Reject Technology Shame," *Atlantic,* November 4, 2015, accessed February 1, 2016, http://www.theatlantic.com/technology/archive/2015/11/whyparentsshouldnt-feel-technology-shame/414163/.
4. Samuel, "Parents."

Chapter 1

1. Sherry Turkle, *Alone Together: Why We Expect More from Technology and Less from Each Other* (New York: Basic Books, 2012).
2. Deborah Roffman, Interview with the author. January 12, 2016.
3. Cindy Pierce, *Sexploitation: Helping Kids Develop Healthy Sexuality in a Porn-Driven World* (Brookline, MA: Bibliomotion, 2015), 38.

Chapter 2

1. James Damico and Mark Baildon, "Examining Ways Readers Engage with Websites During Think-Aloud Sessions," *Journal of Adolescent & Adult Literacy* 51, no. 3 (2007).

2. David Kleeman, "ISpy 2016: Five Things We're Keeping an Eye On," SlideShare, January 11, 2016, accessed February 01, 2016, http://www.slideshare.net/dubit/ispy-2016-five-things-were-keeping-an-eye-on.
3. *#Being13*, produced by Anderson Cooper, 2015.
4. Howard Gardner and Katie Davis, *The App Generation: How Today's Youth Navigate Identity, Intimacy, and Imagination in a Digital World* (New Haven: Yale University Press, 2013), 130–131.

Chapter 3

1. Nichole Dobo, "Parents and Teachers Meet the 'Wild West' When They Try to Find Quality Education Technology," *The Hechinger Report* (2015), accessed March 1, 2016. http://hechingerreport.org/parents-and-teachers-meet-the-wild-west-when-they-try-to-find-quality-education-technology/.
2. Alexandra Samuel, "Parents: Reject Technology Shame," *Atlantic,* November 4, 2015, accessed February 1, 2016, http://www.theatlantic.com/technology/archive/2015/11/whyparentsshouldnt-feel-technology-shame/414163/.
3. Ana Homayoun, "The Dark Side of Teen Sleepovers," *Huffington Post,* June 28, 2014, accessed February 01, 2016, http://www.huffingtonpost.com/ana-homayoun/the-dark-side-of-teen-sle_b_5223620.html.

Chapter 4

1. Howard Gardner and Katie Davis, *The App Generation: How Today's Youth Navigate Identity, Intimacy, and Imagination in a Digital World* (New Haven: Yale University Press, 2013).
2. Gardner and Davis, *The App Generation.*
3. Marina Bers, "Young Programmers—Think Playgrounds, Not Playpens," TEDx Jackson, November 15, 2015, http://www.tedxjackson.com/talks/young-programmers-think-playgrounds-not-playpens/.
4. Marina Umaschi Bers, *Designing Digital Experiences for Positive Youth Development: From Playpen to Playground.* (New York: Oxford University Press, 2012), 29.

Chapter 5

1. "When a School Has a Sexting Scandal," *Note to Self,* WNYC, accessed January 30, 2016, http://www.wnyc.org/story/why-care-about-sexting/.
2. Mathew Ingram, "Snooping on Your Kids: What I Learned About My Daughter, and How It Changed Our Relationship," *Gigaom*, August 8, 2013, accessed April 17 2015, http://gigaom.com/2013/08/08/snooping-on-your-kids-what-i-learned-about-my-daughter-and -how-it-changed-our-relationship/.
3. Dan Szymborski, 2013, comment on Mathew Ingram, "Snooping on Your Kids: What I Learned About My Daughter, and How It Changed Our Relationship."
4. Dannielle Owens-Reid and Kristin Russo, *This Is a Book for Parents of Gay Kids: A Question & Answer Guide to Everyday Life* (New York: Chronicle Books, 2015).
5. Sherry Turkle, *Reclaiming Conversation: The Power of Talk in a Digital Age* (New York: Penguin, 2015), 115.
6. Turkle, *Reclaiming Conversation,* 116.

Chapter 6

1. Jennifer Senior, *All Joy and No Fun: The Paradox of Modern Parenthood* (New York: HarperCollins, 2015), 223.
2. Sherry Turkle, *Reclaiming Conversation: The Power of Talk in a Digital Age* (New York: Penguin, 2015), 117–119.
3. Sherry Turkle, *Alone Together: Why We Expect More from Technology and Less from Each Other* (New York: Basic Books, 2012).
4. Susan Maushart, *The Winter of Our Disconnect: How Three Totally Wired Teenagers (and a Mother Who Slept with Her iPhone) Pulled the Plug on Their Technology and Lived to Tell the Tale.* (New York: Jeremy P. Tarcher/Penguin, 2011).
5. Alexandra Samuel, "Creating a Family Social Media Policy," *Alexandra Samuel* blog, May 26, 2011, accessed January 31, 2016, http://alexandrasamuel.com/parenting/creating-a-family-social-media-policy.
6. Lynn Schofield Clark, *The Parent App: Understanding Families in the Digital Age* (New York: Oxford University Press, 2013), 32.

7. Mike Lanza, *Playborhood: Turn Your Neighborhood into a Place for Play* (Menlo Park, CA: Free Play Press, 2012), 8.

8. Ron Lieber, *The Opposite of Spoiled: Raising Kids Who Are Grounded, Generous, and Smart About Money* (New York: Harper, 2015) 40–41.

Chapter 7

1. Ira Glass, host, *This American Life,* transcript of episode 573: "Status Update," National Public Radio, November 27, 2015, accessed January 31, 2016, http://www.thisamericanlife.org/radio-archives/episode/573/status-update.

2. Glass, *This American Life.*

3. Amanda Lenhart, Monica Anderson, and Aaron Smith, "Teens, Technology and Romantic Relationships," Pew Research Center, October 1, 2015, accessed January 31, 2016, http://www.pewinternet.org/2015/10/01/teens-technology-and-romantic-relationships/.

4. Lenhart, Anderson, and Smith, "Teens, Technology and Romantic Relationships."

5. Lenhart, Anderson, and Smith, "Teens, Technology and Romantic Relationships."

6. Lenhart, Anderson, and Smith, "Teens, Technology and Romantic Relationships."

7. Lenhart, Anderson, and Smith, "Teens, Technology and Romantic Relationships."

8. Lenhart, Anderson, and Smith, "Teens, Technology and Romantic Relationships."

9. Kate Fagan, "Madison Holleran's Friends Share Their Unfiltered Life Stories," ESPN, May 15, 2015, accessed February 1, 2016, http://espn.go.com/espnw/athletes-life/article/12779819/madison-holleran-friends-share-their-unfiltered-life-stories.

10. Devorah Heitner, "Positive Approaches to Digital Citizenship," Discovery Education, September 3, 2015, accessed February 1, 2016, http://blog.discoveryeducation.com/blog/2015/09/03/positive-approaches-to-digital-citizenship/.

11. Devorah Heitner, "Texting Trouble: When Minor Issues Become Major Problems," *Raising Digital Natives*, 2014, accessed January 31, 2016. http://www.raisingdigitalnatives.com/texting-trouble/.

12. Devorah Heitner, "When Texting Goes Wrong," The Family Online Safety Institute blog, June 10, 2014, accessed January 31, 2016, https://www.fosi.org/good-digital-parenting/texting-goes-wrong-helping-kids-repair-resolve/.

13. Glass, *This American Life*.

14. Rachel Simmons, *Odd Girl Out: The Hidden Culture of Aggression in Girls* (New York: Harcourt, 2011).

15. Monica Lewinsky, transcript of TED Talk, "The Price of Shame: Monica Lewinsky," March 2015, accessed January 31, 2016, https://www.ted.com/talks/monica_lewinsky_the_price_of_shame/transcript?language=en.

Chapter 8

1. "Cyberbalance in a Digital Culture," iKeepSafe, 2011–2016, http://ikeepsafe.org/cyberbalance/.

2. "Cyberbalance in a Digital Culture," iKeepSafe.

3. Cathy Davidson, "The Myth of Monotasking," *Harvard Business Review*, November 23, 2011, accessed February 01, 2016, https://hbr.org/2011/11/the-myth-of-monotasking.

4. Nicholas G. Carr, *The Shallows: What the Internet Is Doing to Our Brains* (New York: W.W. Norton, 2010).

5. Robinson Meyer, "To Remember a Lecture Better, Take Notes by Hand," *Atlantic*, May 1, 2014, http://www.theatlantic.com/technology/archive/2014/05/to-remember-a-lecture-better-take-notes-by-hand/361478/.

6. Lecia Bushak, "Why We Should All Start Reading Paper Books Again," *Medical Daily*, January 11, 2015, accessed February 1, 2016, http://www.medicaldaily.com/e-books-are-damaging-your-health-why-we-should-all-start-reading-paper-books-again-317212.

7. Annie Murphy Paul, "You'll Never Learn," *Slate*, May 3, 2013, accessed January 31, 2016, http://www.slate.com/articles/health

_and_science/science/2013/05/multitasking_while_studying
_divided_attention_and_technological_gadgets.html.

8. Alex Soojung-Kim Pang, *The Distraction Addiction: Getting the Information You Need and the Communication You Want, Without Enraging Your Family, Annoying Your Colleagues, and Destroying Your Soul* (New York: Little, Brown and Company, 2013).

9. Pang, *The Distraction Addiction.*

10. Howard Gardner and Katie Davis, *The App Generation: How Today's Youth Navigate Identity, Intimacy, and Imagination in a Digital World* (New Haven: Yale University Press, 2013).

Chapter 9

1. Ruby Karp, "I'm 15 and Snapchat Makes Me Feel Awful About Myself," *Mashable*, October 20, 2015, accessed April 21, 2016, http://mashable.com/2015/10/20/snapchat-teen-insecurity/#fTYTJpk065qj.

2. Karp, "I'm 15 and Snapchat Makes Me Feel Awful."

3. *Sexy Baby*, directed by Ronna Gradus and Jill Bauer, 2012.

4. Susannah Stern, telephone interview by author, January 22, 2016.

5. danah boyd, *It's Complicated: The Social Lives of Networked Teens* (New Haven: Yale University Press, 2015).

6. boyd, *It's Complicated.*

7. Adam Wells, "PSU OL Coach Drops Recruit over Tweets," *Bleacher Report*, July 30, 2014, accessed January 31, 2016, http://bleacherreport.com/articles/2146596-penn-state-ol-coach-herb-hand-drops-recruit-over-social-media-actions?utm_source=cnn.com.

References

Bers, Marina Umaschi. *Designing Digital Experiences for Positive Youth Development: From Playpen to Playground*. New York: Oxford University Press, 2012.

boyd, danah. *It's Complicated: The Social Lives of Networked Teens*. Yale University Press, 2015.

Bushak, Lecia. "Why We Should All Start Reading Paper Books Again." *Medical Daily*. January 11, 2015. Accessed January 31, 2016. http://www.medicaldaily.com/e-books-are-damaging-your -health-why-we-should-all-start-reading-paper-books-again-317212.

Carr, Nicholas G. *The Shallows: What the Internet Is Doing to Our Brains*. New York: W.W. Norton, 2010.

Chua, Amy. *Battle Hymn of the Tiger Mother*. New York: Penguin Press, 2011.

Clark, Lynn Schofield. *The Parent App: Understanding Families in the Digital Age*. New York: Oxford University Press, 2013.

Damico, James, and Mark Baildon. "Examining Ways Readers Engage with Websites During Think-Aloud Sessions." *Journal of Adolescent & Adult Literacy* 51, no. 33 (2007): 254–63.

Davidson, Cathy. "The Myth of Monotasking." *Harvard Business Review*, November 23, 2011. Accessed January 31, 2016. https:// hbr.org/2011/11/the-myth-of-monotasking.

Fagan, Kate. "Madison Holleran's Friends Share Their Unfiltered Life Stories." ESPN, May 15, 2015. Accessed February 1, 2016.

http://espn.go.com/espnw/athletes-life/article/12779819/madison-holleran-friends-share-their-unfiltered-life-stories.

Gardner, Howard, and Katie Davis. *The App Generation: How Today's Youth Navigate Identity, Intimacy, and Imagination in a Digital World.* New Haven: Yale University Press, 2013.

Glass, Ira. "This American Life 573: 'Status Update' Transcript." National Public Radio, November 27, 2015. January 31, 2016.

Guernsey, Lisa, and Michael H. Levine. *Tap, Click, Read: Growing Readers in a World of Screens.* San Francisco: Jossey-Bass, 2015.

Heitner, Devorah. "Positive Approaches to Digital Citizenship." Discovery Education, September 3, 2015. Accessed January 31, 2016. http://blog.discoveryeducation.com/blog/2015/09/03/positive-approaches-to-digital-citizenship/.

———. "Texting Trouble: When Minor Issues Become Major Problems." *Raising Digital Natives,* 2014. Accessed January 31, 2016. http://www.raisingdigitalnatives.com/texting-trouble/.

———. "When Texting Goes Wrong: Helping Kids Repair and Resolve Issues." Family Online Safety Institute, June 10, 2014. Accessed January 31, 2016. https://www.fosi.org/good-digital-parenting/texting-goes-wrong-helping-kids-repair-resolve/#.

Homayoun, Ana. "The Dark Side of Teen Sleepovers." *The Huffington Post.* June 28, 2014. Accessed February 01, 2016. http://www.huffingtonpost.com/ana-homayoun/the-dark-side-of-teen-sle_b_5223620.html.

———. *That Crumpled Paper Was Due Last Week: Helping Disorganized and Distracted Boys Succeed in School and Life.* New York: Penguin Group, 2010.

Kleeman, David. "ISpy 2016: Five Things We're Keeping an Eye On." SlideShare, January 11, 2016. Accessed February 01, 2016. http://www.slideshare.net/dubit/ispy-2016-five-things-were-keeping-an-eye-on.

———. Telephone interview by author, January 18, 2016.

Lanza, Mike. *Playborhood: Turn Your Neighborhood into a Place for Play*. Menlo Park, CA: Free Play Press, 2012.

Lareau, Annette. *Unequal Childhoods: Class, Race, and Family Life*. Berkeley: University of California Press, 2003.

Lathram, Bonnie, Carri Schneider, and Tom Vander Ark. *Smart Parents: Parenting for Powerful Learning*. Elfrig Publishing, 2016.

Lenhart, Amanda, Monica Anderson, and Aaron Smith. "Teens, Technology and Romantic Relationships." Pew Research Center, October 1, 2015. Accessed January 31, 2016.

Lewinsky, Monica. Transcript of TED Talk, "The Price of Shame," March 2015. Accessed January 31, 2016. https://www.ted.com/talks/monica_lewinsky_the_price_of_shame/transcript?language=en.

Lieber, Ron. *The Opposite of Spoiled: Raising Kids Who Are Grounded, Generous, and Smart About Money*. New York: Harper, 2015.

Maushart, Susan. *The Winter of Our Disconnect: How Three Totally Wired Teenagers (and a Mother Who Slept with Her iPhone) Pulled the Plug on Their Technology and Lived to Tell the Tale*. New York: Jeremy P. Tarcher/Penguin, 2011.

Meyer, Robinson. "To Remember a Lecture Better, Take Notes by Hand." *Atlantic*, May 1, 2014. http://www.theatlantic.com/technology/archive/2014/05/to-remember-a-lecture-better-take-notes-by-hand/361478/.

Owens-Reid, Dannielle. *This Is a Book for Parents of Gay Kids: A Question & Answer Guide to Everyday Life*. New York: Chronicle Books, 2014.

Pang, Alex Soojung-Kim. *The Distraction Addiction: Getting the Information You Need and the Communication You Want without Enraging Your Family, Annoying Your Colleagues, and Destroying Your Soul*. New York: Little, Brown and Company, 2013.

Paul, Annie Murphy. "You'll Never Learn." *Slate*, May 3, 2013. Accessed January 31, 2016. http://www.slate.com/articles/

health_and_science/science/2013/05/multitasking_while
_studying_divided_attention_and_technological_gadgets.html.

Pierce, Cindy. *Sexploitation: Helping Kids Develop Healthy Sexuality
in a Porn-Driven World.* Brookline, MA: Bibliomotion, 2015.

Roffman, Deborah M. *Talk to Me First: Everything You Need to
Know to Become Your Kids' Go-to Person About Sex.* Boston: Da
Capo Lifelong, 2012.

————. Telephone interview by author, January 20, 2016.

Samuel, Alexandra. "Creating a Family Social Media Policy." *Alexandra
Samuel* blog, May 26, 2011. Accessed January 31, 2016. http://alex-
andrasamuel.com/parenting/creating-a-family-social-media-policy.

————. "Parents: Reject Technology Shame." *The Atlantic,* November 4, 2015. Accessed February 01, 2016. http://www.theatlantic
.com/technology/archive/2015/11/whyparentsshouldnt-feel
-technology-shame/414163/.

Seiter, Ellen. *Television and New Media Audiences.* Oxford: Claren-
don Press, 1998.

Senior, Jennifer. *All Joy and No Fun: The Paradox of Modern Parenthood.* New York: Harper Collins, 2015.

Sexy Baby. Directed by Ronna Gradus and Jill Bauer. 2012.

Simmons, Rachel. *Odd Girl Out: The Hidden Culture of Aggression
in Girls.* New York: Harcourt, 2011.

Stern, Susannah. Telephone interview by author. January 22, 2016.

Turkle, Sherry. *Alone Together: Why We Expect More from Technology
and Less from Each Other.* New York: Basic Books, 2012.

Turkle, Sherry. *Reclaiming Conversation.* New York: Penguin Press, 2015.

Wells, Adam. "PSU OL Coach Drops Recruit over Tweets." *Bleacher
Report,* July 30, 2014. Accessed January 31, 2016. http://
bleacherreport.com/articles/2146596-penn-state-ol-coach-herb
-hand-drops-recruit-over-social-media-actions?utm_source=
cnn.com.

Index

About the Author

Devorah Heitner, PhD founded **Raising Digital Natives** to serve as a resource for organizations and families wishing to cultivate a culture of thoughtful digital citizenship. She co-authored the *Connecting Wisely in the Digital Age* curriculum and her writing has appeared in the *New York Times*, *Edutopia*, and *PBS Kids*. Dr. Heitner has a PhD in Media, Technology and Society from Northwestern University and has taught at DePaul University, Street Level Youth Media, and Northwestern University. A frequent speaker at national and international schools and conferences, Dr. Heitner lives with her family in Chicago.